Awaken THE **LIGHT** WITHIN YOUR *Heart*

A GUIDE TO SELF-HEALING

SUSAN KENNARD

with Channeled Teachings from
her Council of Light

BALBOA.PRESS
A DIVISION OF HAY HOUSE

Balboa Press books may be ordered through booksellers or by contacting:

Balboa Press
A Division of Hay House
1663 Liberty Drive
Bloomington, IN 47403
www.balboapress.co.uk
UK TFN: 0800 0148647 (Toll Free inside the UK)
UK Local: (02) 0369 56325 (+44 20 3695 6325 from outside the UK)

Print information available on the last page.

ISBN: 978-1-9822-8647-7 (sc)
ISBN: 978-1-9822-8649-1 (hc)
ISBN: 978-1-9822-8648-4 (e)

Balboa Press rev. date: 10/10/2022

My gratitude goes to my two beautiful children,
Sara and Martin, who have taught me so much more
about life, love, and patience than any degrees I have gained.

CONTENTS

PREFACE

Dear Soul,

I welcome you to the next part of your soul's journey.

I am so glad that you chose to go on this journey of healing and discovery. I know that you are going to expand and grow as you listen to and feel the healing codes channelled in this book.

I was guided to share the information throughout this book and guidance to assist you towards healing yourself on a profound level. The processes allow you to release unwanted childhood trauma, limiting beliefs, and old energies holding you back, including past lives that you have brought in with you to heal in this time. In doing this, you are shifting to new timelines. Your mission will become much easier for you to accomplish when you are sparkling brightly, igniting your light, and awakening your gifts. These gifts are part of your soul's plan. By remembering them, you feel not only peace but also a presence that can be explained only as a deep knowing.

I have channelled a statement to clear your energy on a daily basis. I use it every day when I go to sleep and work with my clients, and of course when I was writing this book.

I recommend that you do the Earth Star*Soul Star process to feel grounded and connected before you do any other processes.

Trust that you are guided by your very own team of guides and angels.

Enjoy each process. Feel the activations and light codes flow through you as you read this divinely guided book.

In deep gratitude with much love to you,
Susan and the Guides

INTRODUCTION

We are in the midst of massive global change. And while so many unknowns lie ahead for humanity, it's clear we all have an opportunity to heal and step fully into the life we came to lead. In fact, it's *necessary* for us to do this inner work so that we can show up and create the monumental change this world is craving and needing.

Awaken the Light Within helps readers do this with ease. This book is written for those who want to understand themselves more deeply and to heal on a profound level. It teaches the reader to remember who each of us is: a soul choosing to have a human experience. It guides the reader to align to their divine mission and in doing so to live an abundant life with harmonious relationships.

The profound yet easy-to-follow process outlined in this book guides readers in releasing blocks from the past—whether these may be from childhood, past lives, or their ancestral lines—and awaken the light within their own hearts. Once ignited, this light allows us to step forward to fully align with our mission, activate the intuitive inner guidance we need, and become the people we were meant to be—the people this world needs during this transformational time.

When we are held energetically captive by the past, our potential is severely limited, and we are often prevented from living in freedom, which is our sovereign birthright. We often struggle in our health, our relationships, our access to resources, and much more. Our perceptions and limiting beliefs lead us to choose mediocre lives and experiences, accept less than our true worth, and muffle the voice of our inner guidance. We struggle to see clearly the path meant for us and end up stuck in dead-end and unfulfilling situations that keep us from shining our essential light into the world, being of service in our chosen mission here, and experiencing the joy that is our birth right.

What makes *Awaken the Light Within* unique and important is that it weaves together the latest knowledge about trauma healing with a clear step-by-step process that readers can do on their own for profound and lasting transformation. Literally lifetimes of limitation can be cleared in *minutes* using this method. Never before has it been this simple and transformational to heal the pain of the past. The book weaves in healing codes and channelling from my team of guides, adding potency and support for readers' experiences by elevating their vibration. It also includes numerous success stories in the form of testimonials from people who have experienced tremendous benefit in utilizing this light-awakening process to live their true mission here on Earth.

The book opens with three chapters about my simple upbringing and the story of my personal awakening and healing journey. This was the catalyst to my mission to help others heal and awaken the light within their hearts.

The guides speak throughout Part Two, offering insight into many subjects that we encounter throughout our lives, such as relationships, money, freedom, and even animals and how they help us to heal. Each word that is written in this book is encoded with love and healing; and I hope you will be open to receiving this as you read.

In Part Three, we experience the powerful processes that were channelled to me many years ago whilst working with early childhood trauma, veterans with PTSD, sexual abuse, shocks, and those with dis-ease.

From there, I guide you in using the step-by-step, easy-to-follow processes to clear the past trauma and the pain to heal.

Here is an overview of what to expect with these transformative processes.

The **Earth Star/Soul Star** process (Chapter 17) is activated in order to feel safe, supported, and able to connect to Mother Earth or Gaia and to the universe to align to and manifest our mission here on Earth.

Colour Energy Clearing (Chapter 18) helps us to bypass thought and conscious knowing to get to the core level of trauma to heal, using colour. A chart of the emotional meanings of colour is provided.

The Emotional Wall (Chapter 19) takes us to the origin point of our seeming separation from Source/God/Universe in this lifetime, even if we don't have conscious awareness of this moment. Clearing this trauma re-establishes connection to universal support, and we begin to feel safer and freer in the world.

Time Travelling (Chapter 20) takes us on a journey of healing our inner child so that we can access and clear old feelings that have lingered in our vibrational field throughout the events of life.

The Projector process (Chapter 21) guides us to take an unwanted emotion from our body and place it in front of us to allow a hidden inner child to heal emotionally.

Cutting the Ties That Bind with Forgiveness (Chapter 22) is a powerful relationship-healing and releasing process, and allows you even to cut past ties across lifetimes.

The Mirror process (Chapter 23) guides us to step fully into our light body and truly own our I Am presence through the higher self/light body, which is crucial to stepping into pure abundance and mission.

Soul Rebirthing (Chapter 24) takes us on a journey from conception, growing in the womb, to birth order to heal past lives, epigenetics from our ancestors, and the imprints of our mother's and father's energy on us, allowing us to recreate the blueprint of our soul's mission.

Infinity process (Chapter 25) may be used to visualise and quickly clear energy with a person, situation, or place.

The Forgiveness letter (Chapter 26) is a healing letter you may address to your inner child and your angels.

When we are out of alignment with our mission, we can experience fear, financial lack, sabotage, stuck-ness and even physical disease. *Awaken the Light Within* is the answer to healing the blocks and stepping into our mission.

I will begin by telling you a bit about my story and how I became who I am today, including being a channel and medium. It is my intention to share my story so that you can understand the journey I went on with my family and upbringing. Throughout the book, I will share with you how trauma affects us and how you can connect the dots to understand why we can feel stuck on the path we chose. Testimonials from my clients about their real-life experiences with the healing processes I created will show how you too can heal your own patterns.

It is my intention to reach you all: those who have experienced trauma, those who feel that they want to transform and expand their consciousness, those who want to heal their lives and be the best version of themselves, and those who truly want to remember who they are and to be the light in the world as we all serve our purpose.

PART ONE

MY LIFE'S JOURNEY

1

The Girl from the Village

My spiritual awakening came at the age of 27 years. I didn't know then that my soul had a pre-birth plan and that I had chosen my parents, place of birth, how I was born, and the soul plan of experiencing all that I did. Chapter 3 explores my soul's plan, and Chapter 10, "The Soul's Mission," will cover knowledge that I know will help you truly heal and forgive all those who may appear to have wronged you.

I grew up in a tiny village called Westfield, just outside of Hastings in the south-east of the UK, in a detached house with lots of land. I lived there with my mum, dad, brother, and Nan, my mum's mum who lived in the house attached.

It was a big house almost split in two. My Nan lived literally across the corridor, and as you opened her door, you stepped into her lounge and big kitchen. I can see it so clearly when I think about it now. Whilst growing up, I spent a lot of time with her. Her main front door was old and green and had a big old key to lock it, but to be honest we hardly ever locked the doors in those days—we didn't feel we needed to. My brother and I used to build dens, have secret clubs, and climb trees in the orchard. I used to eat the peas out of the pods in the garden, and dance and sing in the garden of flowers, especially the sweet peas. The house was always full of people, knocking to play or just popping in to say hello.

We were known for our large firework displays and friends and family came to join in. I always watched from the large lounge window, as I was pretty scared of them. Still not sure to this day whether I like them, apart maybe from the sparkles that light up the sky. I never really liked sparklers, either, but wearing gloves I occasionally held one or two. I remember my grandad—Dad's dad—being very silly with them, and these days we would have said he was a health and safety nightmare, but Mum kept him under control by handing out the fireworks one at a time from a metal biscuit tin they were kept in.

My brother loved the big bonfire we always had, and everything we didn't want any longer was thrown onto it. Of course, we always made a guy to stick on the top for the fifth of November, as is British tradition. I was always worried about any animals or insects that might have been living in the mound over the weeks, but Mum always said that as soon as they had heard the fire, they would have left. I so hope she was right.

I was very intuitive as a child, and Mum said she used to see me talking and singing down the garden. I was in a world of my own. Maybe I was talking to nature spirits, or just my guides—who knows. I think that I must have shut my connection down, as it really wasn't spoken about then. This disconnect can happen with children when the connection is not acknowledged by adults, or if we experience trauma and shock as children. As a soul, we would have chosen everything, so there is no blame.

No one in my family ever spoke about "spirit" or the afterlife, so I just lived my life as a child not really thinking too much about it. In fact, most families still don't talk about children's psychic abilities, even though more and more children are letting us know that they are connected and more in tune than we ever were. Mine certainly are.

I was a daddy's girl for a long time. My dad used to have a shed—I am smiling as I type this—where he used to spend lots of his time, playing with the model railway he had created himself. He was mad on trains. I remember him being out of the house pretty much most of the time. He drove a long-distance lorry, delivering pet food at one point, and I occasionally went to work with him. I remember the Guinness advert that featured a toucan—I was excited to meet him one day. From that day on, I have always loved talking birds, as does my son, Martin.

Mum looked after us at home and also worked as a dinner lady at Westfield School, which was the local school we attended. She had gone there too, and so did her mum, so it held history. She still talks about it to this day.

Mum told me she did that job so she could look after us and work at the same time. She also worked in the fruit fields, picking apples, strawberries, and raspberries. She always looked like she had just come back from the Bahamas, but of course it was from being outside in the sun all day with little shade. I seem to remember on occasion going too so I could earn some pocket money in the holidays. I really didn't like it and used to go to sleep imagining picking raspberries. I would dream about them and wake up, seeing them in my mind.

The environment we are brought up in really does create part of who we are. The beliefs we hold can come from many experiences, but the earliest ones are almost like a blueprint to our lives later on. The way we saw the world is sometimes how we view the world now, and how we bring our children up too.

Mum always worried about money, but from a child's perspective we had everything we needed and more. I grew up confused about money, as there was so much discussion around it. I can still see my mum rooting around in the sofa for change that my dad might have dropped. There were arguments at the table around the lack of money. Saying "money doesn't grow on trees" was mentioned daily to say we couldn't afford something. I don't remember ever going without, so I understand the confusion when I look at it now. I think it was just old fear. Nan had my mum when she was in her forties—unheard of then, as older mums were out of the ordinary.

But Nan was a war baby and so, I feel, held lot of fear of lack because of rationing when she was growing up.

Saying that, I always felt safe with Nan and spent many an hour with her teaching me knitting and crocheting. I quickly found out that I was much better making things and sewing, as I just couldn't get the hang of knit one, miss one, or whatever it was.

In her bedroom, Nan had a big old chest of drawers which held lots of bits and pieces I could cut up, stick, and glue. I made all sorts of things from virtually nothing. Every time I was called a clever clogs. It's funny how these things stick in our minds, and how I do the same now with my own children. We are always sticking and gluing, and my son Martin—who is 8 at the time of this writing—is very good at sewing.

I hope the stories and messages I've written about my life in this first part of the book can show how it unfolded for me to become the person I am today, living my mission and loving myself. As I write this book for you, it's my intention to blend my professional experience with my channelled guidance so that you, the reader, can understand that it truly is possible to heal. Through the processes offered, I know that you will start to see both a transformation within your inner self as you let go of old trauma and the shift in your external world. I know you will feel so much more connected to your soul's plan, and perhaps even remember why you chose your mission and what you were meant to do in this lifetime.

Healing is not a quick fix; it is a journey with compassion that starts with you. I will start by sharing my spiritual awakening.

2

Martin and My Awakening

At 27 years old, I was awoken in the early hours of morning by a telephone call. It was a girl telling me that a dear friend of mine, a previous boyfriend, had taken his life. She said that she was his girlfriend and that she had found the Christmas card from me to him with my number and wanted to let me know.

I thanked her for letting me know, but only after the call ended did it sink in. Lots of emotions and thoughts. Maybe I could have helped. Why didn't he let me know? And the big question: why? This was a man who appeared to have it all. On paper, he did. His parents were wealthy, he wanted for nothing, and he had his own pizza franchise.

But he had told me that his girlfriend had become pregnant and that he had made her have an abortion. I think that was one of the reasons he left—he couldn't cope with the guilt and regretted it.

I was devastated. Martin had been so important in my life that I later chose to name my son after him. He had been living in his home country of New Zealand, and because it was on the other side of the world, I couldn't go to the funeral. At the time, I was finishing my postgraduate degree in psychotherapy and living in London, working as a nanny for two young children. The parents worked for BBC radio and were amazingly supportive.

Then it happened: I had been getting on with my life, as you do, when one night, a few months after I had received the news about Martin, I was woken again, this time by a feeling that someone was in the room. I sensed the presence of someone, and a dog too. I was asleep and yet awake. I couldn't move. I could see but not through my eyes—with an inner vision. I felt someone touch my shoulder gently, shaking me as if to wake me up. I admit I was scared in that moment, as I had never experienced anything like that. It was surreal yet profound. As quickly as it had come, it was gone. I did not know at this point that it was Martin and his sausage dog, who had passed six months before he had.

Since then, Martin has visited me many times. But for days after this first visit—or it may have actually been months—I found it hard to sleep. The last thing I wanted was for that to happen again. I slept with the light on and the radio on a timer, as I just didn't want to be on my own.

I had a friend whom I had told about what had happened. He decided to gift me a reading. I had never had one before, and the scientist within me wanted to see what it was all about. The medium came to visit me. She sat with me and started to tell me so much information about Martin: what he looked like, his obsession with his hair (which he said was receding), our holidays travelling New Zealand, and our party times. She knew intricate details about where we had stayed and what we had done together—from jet skiing to looking at the stars at his parents' beach house in Pauanui. No one knew these things apart from Martin and me.

I was so surprised. With floods of tears down my cheeks, I knew that she was giving evidence of survival. That Martin was really talking to her. She said that he was proud of me and had come to let me know that he was fine that night. He didn't mean to scare me, and I should remember to shine like a star. He would be with me and support me.

Then right at the end of the reading, she looked at my hands and said, "Oh, by the way, this is your journey too. You are a natural medium."

I laughed. I told her I was a psychologist and had no intention of being a medium. She just smiled.

A few months later, during a stressful period of my postgraduate training, I needed to quieten my mind. I kept seeing signs for meditation, specifically transcendental meditation. I saw them everywhere. One day I was reading a magazine on the tube train and saw an article on TM held at the Marishi Yogi centre in Baker Street, London. Something told me to contact them. It was quite a lot of money for a student, but as I know now, when something is meant to be, the universe always lines up for us.

I contacted the centre, and they offered me a big discount and the ability to pay monthly for the training. I had read the research, and there seemed to be so much evidence to say that productivity improved and so did clarity of mind. I decided sign up for it. I didn't know exactly how important this course would be in my life.

From the day I started to meditate, my whole world opened up. I started to know when things were about to happen, the world seemed brighter, and my tutor even noticed the quality of my essays had changed. She actually asked if I had written them, as they were of such greater clarity and quality.

As time went on, I qualified in psychoanalytic psychotherapy at the Tavistock Centre in North London and took a job in child protection as a trauma specialist. As a person with a scientific brain, I needed evidence, so it took me a really long while before I accepted that I was a medium. I spent months researching guides, spirits, and mediumship, and then finally after an invite to a workshop, I found myself at the College of Psychic Studies in Kensington, studying psychic development and later learning, with resistance, to be a medium. I was blessed to have been taught by the best.

Learning to use my gift professionally was one of the best things I ever did. Today I teach professional channelling, and I help people heal themselves on a deep cellular level. My mission is to help you align to yours. Healing ourselves is the key to aligning to our missions—after all, mission equals love. Being happy is something that happens naturally when we are truly living our mission, being of service, and loving ourselves.

The journey as a medium led me to lead a double life. I was working as a specialist in trauma within the field of child protection, and working on the stages in London as a channel and medium. I didn't know then that this was part of my soul's plan, but it all makes sense, as speaking publicly is something I love, especially with my guides by my side as my channels for healing and teaching. All of this led me towards the journey of truly living my mission to help others align and live theirs. I realise how blessed I am to have my guides by my side, nudging me when needed. Once you open the door to your guides, there is no closing it. They are just as excited that you remembered you are not on your own as you will be to know it.

A few years and many courses, modalities, and healing journeys later, I found myself truly knowing that we are a soul in a body having a human experience. Our minds and bodies are completely interconnected with our souls, and there is no separation. I realised that psychotherapy, or talking therapy, was just one way of understanding the human journey, not the only way. To help me explore further the nudge I received from my guides, I decided to train as a naturopath at the College of Natural Nutrition. What a profound healing journey it was to learn that another way we can heal ourselves is through foods and cleansing techniques. This knowledge stays with me today, and I still use the techniques, such as Epsom salt baths and skin brushing, to help my clients understand how to look after their physical bodies from the inside out.

The guides told me a long time ago that our bodies are the barometers for the soul and that they are always talking to us. This is something I am passionate about teaching. Another eye-opening training that took healing to another level for me was Meta health, incorporating science and the spiritual.

3

My Soul's Plan

To travel back a little and to give you an insight into more of my soul's plan, I will share a little more of my personal journey.

In 2006, I found myself drawn to lectures and watching mediums at the Spiritual Association of Great Britain (SAGB) in Victoria, London. It was here that at the age of 36 I met a man who was to become the father of my children.

I was guided to enrol myself in a trance mediumship class. The whole aspect of letting go of control scared me, but for some reason I was drawn to give it a go. In trance mediumship, you allow a spirit to step into your body and speak through you. The teacher—I will call Jack—was an amazing teacher and an amazing channel. I learned so much from him in such a short time—the main thing being that there was nothing to be scared of with spirits.

Time went on, and Jack and I decided to do some work together. I can't remember exactly how it happened now, but I felt divinely guided to do it. We ended up getting together and entered into a relationship. It was a whirlwind for sure: within three weeks he asked me to marry him, and within three months we had a beautiful surprise on the way. He was over the moon with the news of a baby, and I was in shock. That was over ten years ago as I write, and our daughter has grown up to be an incredible blessing, as is our son who is growing fast. I will share with you the main parts to this, as it led to an incredible spiritual awakening and a profound journey of taking responsibility for what I had chosen and attracted into my life experience and the soul's unique plan.

Going back many years, Jack and I had a challenging relationship, but it wasn't all bad. Eventually we decided to part ways and end the relationship. At the time, making this decision was not easy. As our relationship was breaking down, I remember a time before I found the strength and courage to ask him to leave when I was crying, sitting on my bed, pregnant with my son, with my daughter in her cot asleep. In my mind's eye, I saw Nan, mums mum who had passed years earlier, and lots of blue lights to the right of me. I knew that I was being guided and that I was not on my own, but it wasn't the right time. I knew there must be a very important reason I needed to experience this, one that would become clear as time went on.

This was probably one the most difficult times I have ever experienced. Around this same time, my mum had been diagnosed with cancer and told she had three months to live. I am happy to say they were wrong, and thirteen years later she is still here.

Looking back and reflecting, I know that this man agreed to come into my life to help me to shine my light. He and I together chose all of what we experienced to grow our own soul's path and journey. Without this emotional experience of being on my own with two children and having to reinvent myself, I know my service to humanity would have been very different. There is nothing like providing for two babies financially, emotionally, and spiritually to focus your energy. They were my push to success and to being the light in the world that I truly love being.

I have forgiven myself and Jack. I understand the soul's journey, I understand his part in my expansion, and I get why it was so challenging. As I write, I haven't yet met the man to share my life and dreams with, but I know that when the universe aligns us, we will meet. Maybe by the time you are reading this book, our souls and paths will have aligned.

PART TWO

THE GUIDES

4

Loving Yourself, and How to Heal

If you are reading this and feel it's time to find *your* freedom, then I hope the processes I am about to share will help you to heal your relationships and your life. What I do know is that to truly heal, we need to forgive—not just say the words, but feel the letting them go with love.

Forgiveness is the key to compassion. We are one, and as we forgive another, we are forgiving ourselves. There have been many times in childhood when we have felt un-held emotionally, and while this feeling is not the fault of anyone, it is time to give ourselves compassion and heal those un-held parts.

I truly feel that I live a life of abundance and that my journey of healing and expansion has led me to align fully to why I am here. It's time for you to shine your light and heal those unwanted parts that have held you back for so long. Having found this book, in this time of great awakening.

Compassion is key to truly letting go and loving yourself. Many times we have said unkind words to ourselves and berated ourselves, even if this has been unconscious. At a frequency level, our body is hearing every word, as it too holds a vibration. Remember, we are a soul choosing to have a human experience, and our body holds the messages to help us align to our mission. Being uncompassionate to yourself is being unkind to your beautiful body, your vehicle, and ultimately your soul's mission. What words do you say to yourself? Are they loving words such as "you are beautiful," or unkind words such as "you can't possibly be lovable"?

Words are spells, so why not make those spells loving ones?

Loving of the Self

This section is a combination of the guides' words and my interpretation of them. The guides impress what they want me to say, and I use my understanding to interpret what they meant.

We would like to talk to you about how to love yourself. Loving yourself is the fastest way to living the life of your dreams. Those who cannot access love for themselves will never find it in another. Someone else will never provide or fill the space that is there within you.

So let's talk about those spaces, or thinking of it as trauma might be easier to understand. Where do spaces in one's life come from?

A space in one's life and ultimately in one's field comes from an interruption in light. The guides went on to say, "We have spoken about this before, but we wish for you to write this in your book, as it is an important reminder to you all that we are really just energy, just light, and in essence a pure light being.

"You have lived many lifetimes as just light, but those of you, you included, have chosen to volunteer at this time to inhabit a human form, feel emotion, and therefore experience the pain and suffering that so many of you feel you deserve. You volunteered to support and assist in helping others heal and to bring more light to the planet.

"We are here to tell you that there is never a need to experience physical or emotional pain. This may come as a surprise to those reading this information; however, pain—both emotional and physical—is only a message of interruption in light, essentially the lack of love in our field."

So loving ourselves is the fastest way towards finding our own healing path. The question becomes, how do we understand and put into practice loving ourselves?

When you understand the laws of the universe, you will begin to understand where you need to refine your energy field. Transforming your beliefs is the fastest way of refining and lightening your energy field. When we talk about refining, we are talking about healing the interruptions of light that are stopping you from being the best version of your beautiful human-body form that you can be.

To experience this best self, you can access those parts of you that are not in alignment with your mission here. You all chose a mission to complete, and you also chose to be shown in your physical body when you would be out of alignment with your mission—be this pain, weight, illness, or other ill effect. You chose this as an indicator of your alignment.

You have experienced many lifetimes before, many lives, and you have brought aspects of them through this time to heal. You may notice the effects in patterns in this life that you attract, for example in relationships, tiredness, mood, or fear of the future. These are not from today; they resonate along your timeline of experience within your field of light and get triggered though patterns. They show themselves first in the environment—meaning your outside world—you live in, such as your home, your bank account, and your relationships. The outside world is a reflection of our inside world. It's so simple and easy to detect unwanted emotions. It is your job then to access the emotion and clear it from your light field.

We don't have to trawl through the whole of our childhood to find these unwanted emotions, or through our past lives. We can, however, feel them within our body, perhaps give them a colour, acknowledge, and let them go.

Here is an example. Notice when you feel an unwanted feeling. Close your eyes, acknowledge it, feel it in your body, and thank your body for showing you. Fill that space with golden sparkling light. Know that by feeling, acknowledging it, and then letting it go, you can be free of that emotion. Watch how it stops playing out in your life. The processes in this book will help you to go deeper and heal the patterns you hold.

5

Healing Codes from the Light

Our ability to heal ourselves is infinite. We have the power to self-heal, so why do we feel we have to hand our power over to another to heal us? Granted, we definitely need the medical model; the universe has given this way of healing so that in certain circumstances, such as accidents and operations, we can utilise it. However, if we were able to remember that we can heal ourselves, would we visit our doctor as much as we perhaps have in the past?

Here is how my guides responded to these questions.

GUIDES: We want you to remember that you were born with the knowledge that you have infinite power and that you can heal any part of your energy field at any time. We channel this information for you at this time, as we have noticed that fear has over taken many on your planet, and indeed in your society. We want to offer you a simple way to access and heal yourself. Essentially, we would like you to gain back your power and be more fully in alignment with unconditional love.

We are those speaking as the council of light, and we work on a high-vibrational frequency toning through this channel of light.

17

We do this to raise the frequency in your heart field, allowing you the ability to reflect light more readily within your cells. With this brighter reflection, your life reflects back to you in that same high-vibrational light. So essentially your life becomes lighter, your body becomes free, and you are attracted to the pure and abundant opportunities that flood in. You always knew this, as it was part of your purpose to remember who you are.

Those who are reading this are ready to embark on the journey of self-healing. If you can imagine that you are just a light, then as we look at you, we can see any interruptions in your field. We see these interruptions clearly, as does the channel writing this information for you. When you can access the interruptions in your own light field and heal them, you are free. With this new-found freedom, you are fully able to be a bringer of light.

We love you and wish to assist you on your healing journey.

We know that many of you are experiencing great fear in the realms of your planet. We wish you to know that in that moment of realisation, this fear is not real, and the illusion of what you are seeing disappears. So you may ask, why do we feel fear if it's not real? You feel fear because it is part of your emotional body to experience many emotions. You chose to send the feeling to the universe to expand not only your consciousness but the universe exponentially. You chose to allow emotions to flow through you, not inhabit you. This is your learning and expansion.

We are so grateful that you chose to volunteer to be here at this time, to bring your light and raise the vibration of the planet. It was all an experiment—nothing more, nothing less. This does not take away, however, from your experience; just as you came to experience fear, you came to experience unconditional love of yourself. This, we see, you find the hardest task in the human form you chose. We smile as the channel is writing this, as we know that you were so excited to experience all these emotions and see how they affected your physical form. However, now you are present in human form, it is not such an exciting experience. We smile with love and gratitude for the journey you have chosen. It is for us too, and we stand fully by your side at all times.

The channel has struggled with the concept of not being on her own. Many times in her life she has felt she was doing this all on her own. However, now it is clear to her that we are here to help her and assist her with her journey to bring the brightest light for others to follow. She is a leader, and we are helping her to stand fully in her mission to be a lighthouse, you may say, to guide others.

Ego is something we wish to communicate to you. You worry, as does this channel, that you may be coming from ego. What is ego?

Ego is the mind, the human mind connecting with desires and wishes it chose to experience. What you experience is not ego—it is being human. You are just light, and a light that wishes to express itself here on the earth plane. It wishes to expand, and to do this the human ego has to be part. If you feel a desire or wish, then you are being guided, if it is from a place of loving yourself or another.

So now when you doubt yourself and worry that you are coming from ego, remember that without ego you are not human.

Ahh, you say; now I can breathe …

Yes, you truly can.

Breathing is such an important part of your experience on earth. Without the breath, you would not be here. So why is it that you hold your breath, or cover your breath with certain substances and breathe in air that is polluted? The answer again is fear. Your fear your power and your light, so you find a way to dull your light so that you feel safe.

We ask you to breathe light into your body; breathe light into your heart and your soul. When you take in the full breath of light, your life will expand. You will no longer live half your life; you will be the fully expanded version you were meant to be.

Try this simple exercise. Imagine you can see a rainbow ball of light travel down to your heart centre, and feel the love for you, just you, that resides inside.

Now you are connected. Now you can feel your mission. We greet you with our essence and our gratitude for taking this mission for the good of expansion.

This is a daily practice. We wish to connect with you and assist you on your journey.

Blessings from the Council of Light.

Light Codes

Your body is designed to hold the full spectrum of light. When your light field is reflecting enough light, you can see the reflection in your outside world.

You are experiencing more gratitude for your life. You are seeing the beauty in all things, living or otherwise. You are seeing more freedom and experiencing it too. People are loving and kind towards you, and you are noticing this. You can see this when your light field holds the full spectrum of light.

When you are sitting in the sunshine, imagine that you are receiving the full spectrum of light. You can feel the codes coming from the sun. These codes are opening up your cells to receive more light. This is why you feel good when you are on holiday or walking in the sun: you are receiving the healing light from the great central sun of Source. You are receiving healing in your cells and therefore bringing more light into your field.

You have the ability to see the whole spectrum of light in your field. Ask which colour is needed to align to more light. Sit quietly and breathe. Ask your inner knowing, "What colour do I need?" Imagine that colour flooding your cells and your body, and expanding your light. Keep asking until you feel you are holding all the colours. Go to the Colour Energy Clearing process in Chapter 18 and use the chart to look up what the colours mean emotionally for you. Ask for that emotion to be healed, allowing more light to be held.

Healing Steps

Each one of these laser healings will allow you to raise the vibration of your heart field, reflecting back a more beautiful experience to you in human form. Have fun and expect more love and abundance to enter your life.

Emotions and Colours

Imagine a beam of light entering your body from your crown to your feet, filling up every cell. Here is a chart the guides gave me for this book to help you. If you feel these emotions, then imagine the colours as rays of light to diffuse them and heal.

resentment	magenta
judgement	turquoise
fear	pure platinum
guilt	silver
envy	gold
self-doubt	green
more physical energy	rainbow (full spectrum of light)
worry	gold and turquoise
more love	pink and gold

Water

Drinking pure blessed water hydrates your cells. To enhance its healing power, place your hand over the water, seeing light absorb the water and fill with the energy of love.

Epsom salt baths are great for detoxifying—and relaxing too.

There are several ways to clear or enhance your energy field and thereby bring more light into your body and cells. Healing comes from within. People look outside themselves for the answer, but the answer is always found within, not outside.

Those outside you can help and assist you to find the true answer to your own mission, your own healing, and your own journey. Facilitators can help and guide, and can help you to heal yourself. You, and only you, know your true essence, know your true essence—the essence of your soul, your true self.

Now you can hear us, now you can hear that you have all the answers, you will never need doubt again. As you read this book, you can tap into the soul part of you, that part that has all the knowledge within, that part that knows no bounds and is completely perfect in every way.

Universal guidance is your friend; you can heal you. Place your hands on your heart, and trust in the guidance you hear. Ask any question and see what you feel. We are here with you, and we are so excited that you are ready.

This journey that you chose to take was chosen many timelines before—not just this lifetime, but lifetimes before. These times you might not remember consciously, but you will remember as you awaken to the light within your heart. These plans will not go unheard, as your soul knows and never forgets.

When you truly awaken to the light, you will find the joy of life, the peace that you have been searching for—the inner peace that those who have human form are constantly searching for.

Finding the light within your heart is the only way you will find that peace. Not from something or someone outside you but from that true essence of your soul, that part that knows no bounds. It is that part of you that you must connect with and listen to. This is where you will find the all your answers, your insight—your inner knowing, some call it. That sixth sense that you always had.

The question I asked the guides is, "How do we get to that place of inner knowing? How do we achieve nirvana, or indeed the peace within?"

GUIDES: That, my child, is the journey of healing, the journey of healing that child within, that part of you that decided that the world was scary, fearful, all those times you felt on your own. When you heal these parts of you that felt separated from Source/God, you are living in divine order and divine alignment. You are living your life in divine flow. The childhood that you had this time was never the origin of your belief; the origin came from those contracts, past lives, and past experiences of fear. Feeling that you are going to die led you to shut down your unique, perfect connection to God/Source energy. Of course it was never shut; however, the heart walls may have prevented you from hearing.

You are a special soul to us. You are so incredibly loved by us, and we are grateful that you chose to be here and walk the human plane to advance all of our existence, to help us to expand. This is one unified journey. We are all one; we are not me and you, we are us. We always were just us—never you and me and them, but us. Every life you have lived is within you; every emotion you have felt is with you. There is only now: not future, not past, but now. We ask you to live only in the now, only in that part of you that is in perfect alignment with your mission.

Your mission is your chosen path. You sometimes feel as if you are swaying from that path, but truthfully you never are. You chose to remember who you are, you chose to know who you are. Yes, we know you forgot it in your mind and body, but your soul never forgot—your soul always knows.

The time is now, the time now to awaken to the light within your heart. The light you have within you is so bright, brighter than any light you have ever seen with the naked human eye. This light is you: yes, you have a human form as you are reading this; however, truly who you are is light. Those parts of you that you think are wrong or bad are just those fears that are not real. It's always been an illusion, an illusion that you chose to experience so that you could experience emotion.

6

Healing the Body

Your body is the vehicle for your soul. A disclaimer: I do not claim to heal or cure. The guides are conveying their perspective on healing. Read this information and take what resonates for you. Consult a medical practitioner if you feel you need to.

GUIDES: We know that some of you reading this will be taken by illness and dis-ease, taken by your thoughts, taken by beliefs. We ask you to listen to your body. Listen to the answers within.

Not only do we awaken the light within our mind, we awaken to the light within our body. As we do this, we become brighter: our eyes are clear, our skin is glowing, our body heals.

Some may say, "How can that be? By just awakening the light within? Surely I can't heal my body." But when you remember that your soul knows no bounds, that you came into this life to know when your light was dimmed, when you were not in alignment with your divine mission, then you will know that you chose for your body to be a barometer—you chose for your body to let you know. Those aches and pains you feel, those heart palpitations—those are messages that your soul is trying to talk to you. The stiffness of your joints, the unexplained dis-ease that just appeared.

Then you may ask, "But what about children? Why it is that children are seeing these messages, and they are just born?" We would say look to the parents—the parents and the ancestors. We know that this channel loves to talk about the science of the body, and where the origin and brain messages arrive from. If you can imagine that you bring in these beliefs, thoughts, and feelings from times before to heal in this lifetime, it might allow you to let go more easily.

It is not about punishing yourself. It's not about feeling sorry for yourself and shutting yourself away. It's about listening. It's about healing and really hearing what your body is telling you.

If you have been given a diagnosis, try talking to that part of your body, and listen. Love every single cell, organ, part of you. Do not try to kill it, as you are only killing you. Love those cells, love your organs, and love your body. As you awaken the light within, you awaken to greater love of your body.

You will find that you start to choose options that are right for you. These are options that heal your light within and bring more light to your field, not less. These are in perfect alignment for your healing journey.

Do not give up if all else has failed. Do not feel "I have to fix this." Just surrender. When you surrender to the light within, surrender to that inner knowing, that inner part of you that has all the answers that knows no bounds.

We wish to give you an exercise. We wish for you to sit quietly, put your hands on your heart, and close your eyes. Breathe gently in and out a few times. Breathe into the part of your body that is trying to talk to you. Have no judgement, have no attachment. Just listen. Ask your cells, "What do I need to know? What you feel? What you are trying to tell me?"

Ask, "How I can heal you? What do I need to do to heal myself, to bring more light into my body and my field?"

When you hear the words, these words will come from love, pure love. Your inner knowing will be able to guide you to hear the message or messages that your body is trying to tell you.

All messages are telling you that you must love yourself more, that you must love every part of you—not to just say it but to really feel it. Your mind is not separate from body; your soul is not separate from body. You are a unified field of light, just choosing a body at this time. However, you can feel the essence of your light when you sit quietly with your hands on your heart and breathe.

You chose to experience this human form and to breathe. Your breath is the difference from the soul's consciousness; that is the only difference. Without breath and body, you would be just light. Just light and part of the unified field.

Vibration and Frequency

You know that you are part of the unified light field. Light is an energy and a vibration. It was always your job to be aware of your vibration and frequency. To check in with how you feel, take time to do inner work and heal those parts that are not feeling loved and therefore reflecting back to you in your relationships with others. Your relationship with you and the level of joy and abundance you experience.

It is not a matter of just thinking yourself healed; it is changing the amount of light you have and hold in your field. With this transformation of light, you are able to attract that of the reflection of your field. So when you see more love, opportunities, and abundance coming into your life, your bank account, and your bodily changes, then you will know that your field of light has shifted and that you are holding more light in the unified field.

The excitement you feel when you see your life change is such a joy to us. We know that you are remembering more and more, that you are awakening the light within. With this awakening, you will experience so much more alignment to mission, and what goes with this is an expression of your soul. Your soul is expressing itself all the time through your light field, so it's your job to keep bringing more light in. All you need to do is love yourself more and more, remembering who you are: a soul having a human experience. It really is simple. When you chose to do this, it was not from a human expression. You knew that your soul's mission was the important reason for being here and that everything else was not important. Nothing else mattered.

Connect now with your heart by placing your hands over your heart and breathing. As you breathe, you can ask within, "What do I need to know about my mission?" See what you receive. Write it down, and then ask again each day to see what appears to you as a theme.

Your soul is always speaking to you. You just have to listen. When you hear words of love, you know it is your soul's message. If it doesn't feel like love, then it's not your soul talking—it's your mind.

Let's now talk about contrast. When we talk about contrast, we are talking about the darker energies that reside in our field—those that give us contrast in this human experience.

As everything is a reflection, only dark can be attracted to dark, and light to light. Your fears, doubts, shock, contracts, guilt, and shame attract dark energies, so as you raise your vibration to the light, you attract that of the light. It is another indication to remember who you truly are.

Lower or Dark Energies

Dark energies affecting you was another way you chose to know that your light held darker or absent-of-light vibrations such as fear and shame. You might ask what these dark energies are. We bring these in from lifetimes before, from times when we had shock, trauma, accidents, karmic aspects, drug or alcohol use, or other negative events. When you hold shock, then your light has dust in it or is not as light; therefore, it attracts an entity that has the same vibrational frequency. This is how universal attraction works. All of these can contribute to attracting lower energies. Sometimes it is those who have passed but don't know they have passed who are attracted to your light.

So the more light we bring into our field, the more love we hold, and therefore we cannot attract dark energies.

Statement to clear unwanted energies. *Creator all that is, it is commanded that you pull, clear, cancel, and delete on all four levels and resolve on the history level any waywards, watchers, entities and attachments. Also release anyone who needs to return to the light and to unconditional love. It is done, it is done, it is done; thank you, thank you, thank you.*

Fear

GUIDES: We would like to talk to you about fear. We would like to tell you that this fear you feel is a dulling of your light. Fear has come from times before when you have felt separated from your light. You never were separated, but you have felt that separation by shocks, traumas, and beliefs around the outside world and indeed many lifetimes.

When fear or shock is within your field, you are reflecting it back to yourself and therefore your life experience. We can tell you and remind you that there really is nothing to fear in this life, that you are always loved and protected, though there were times that you didn't feel that way. You did not feel safe. Maybe as a child, maybe in previous times. Maybe you brought this in from your ancestors to heal. Whatever or wherever it came from, you can heal this. As you read these words, we are releasing the fear vibration held in your field. We are opening your heart field to receive more love and light. Feel this and know this. Acknowledge that child-self, that baby-self, and let them know that they are loved. As you do this, you are healing that part of you that did not feel loved as a child or didn't feel accepted or important.

(In Part Three, you will find processes to heal that inner child. You will be guided to the perfect one that will help you.)

When you look at your outside world, you can see how much love or how much fear is in your field. Be a witness to your life; see what is around, how you respond to people, things, and situations. Do this without judgement. Do this with love and compassion of yourself and of your journey, and know that all is well, that you are your own healer and you can heal yourself.

Pain in the Body

Pain in the body is your way of knowing that you are in resistance towards something in your life. This resistance is just a part of you that is holding long-standing and deep fear of moving forward. Honour that ache, that pain, that resistance, and ask for your soul to guide you. Bring the message of that pain, that resistance, to the fore. See it, talk to it, feel the emotion or colour, and ask for it be released.

You have the power to move forward in your life, the power to heal yourself and therefore heal your pain. Fear of moving forward can be part of your past experiences of fear of dying. In many times before, you have met your end of your life in a traumatic and fearful way. Ask for all these fear and pain bodies to be released now. Ask for your soul to guide you and show you what you need to heal.

You have the all the answers within. Nothing is hidden, your soul knows no bounds. You are perfect in your light: nothing is wrong, nothing is bad. You are divinely guided at all times. Get into the practice of knowing and remembering that you are always loved and never on your own. We are with you at all times, never far from your thoughts. It is just your beliefs that stop you from healing, stop you from moving on, and stop you from accessing your true abundant life mission.

Connect with the part of the body that is showing the message. Where is it in your physical body? Listen to what your back, your neck, your arm, or your head is telling you. Whatever part of the body is holding the message, know that as you love that part of you, you are bringing more light into your field. You are allowing the full spectrum of light and the full experience of living your mission—your divine flow of abundance. This flow of abundance is always within you. It's yours to have live and experience. If you are listening now to your body, what emotion, what experience, or part of you is feeling the fear of moving forward?

Now let's move on to the emotion. Feel where that is in your body. When you think about a particular situation in your life, what comes up for you? Do you feel in control of your life? Do you feel that you have lost your power? We are here to tell you that you have power within that is beyond anything you could even imagine. You are part of the unified field, and the field is expansive.

You can tap into the field that you are at any time. See yourself in the life you want, see yourself in the body you want, free from illness, pain, excess weight. See yourself in the loving relationship that you desire. This is all in the unified field that is you.

- Place your hands on your heart, close your eyes, and breathe …
- Visualise yourself in your ideal space, ideal life, ideal love, and connect with that part of you that is the light that you are.
- See a bubble of light in front of you; see yourself in this bubble in the life you desire.
- Smile with every cell of your body; smile in your heart, smile with your whole being.
- Bring that bubble of your vision into your heart. Know that as you do this, you create that in your field.
- Now feel whether you have any resistance; if you do, ask for the fear to be released. There is only fear or love, so we can keep this simple.

You may feel this in your body, or you may get a thought in your mind. Just acknowledge and let it go. Ask and it is given. Hand it over to Source. Feel that happiness and love flow through every cell of your body.

Food

GUIDES: Food is such a subject for you, we know. Which foods are right for you? We ask you to feel into the foods you choose; we ask you to bless the food you put into your body; we ask you love the food you put into your body. With these three things, you are able to feel what is right for you.

The answers are within, not without. No person having a human experience will be the same. On this earth there are many trying to help others to be healthy. Still, the answers are within. No diet or way of eating will heal you on its own—the healing comes from the light you hold in your cells. You know that the vibration of the food is the key to absorbing the nutrients necessary for health of your physical form, so you can transform that vibration by sending your light into the food. You can send your love and gratitude and light into every food you put into your body. Your body is light, and your human form holds the messages for your soul. Your soul knows exactly what it needs to eat. It knows what is perfect for this human form you chose. *The answers are within.*

As for beliefs around medicine, we know that on your earth this is a subject spoken about frequently. We know that this subject has long-held beliefs and that some live by these. It is for you to know that all healing comes from within.

When seeking for something to fix our problem, we are seeking outside the soul's consciousness and soul's knowing. We are seeking in the place that is out of the unified field of light. If you were to know that all healing comes from within, you would know that you truly can heal yourself. No one, no medicine, and nothing outside you can heal you—just love and light alone. However, if you believe a medicine will heal you and you take it without fear, then you are bringing a different frequency into your body.

You know that on your earth there is something called a "placebo" and that this experimental way of healing often will work. The reason for the placebo is to show you that with the thought you can heal. You thought that you were being given something that healed you, so you believed it. As you believed it, you let go. You brought more light into your field, more love, and became one with the unified field.

So you see why we are talking to you about this. We want you to remember that you have all the answers within. You are the one with the only answer to your body's message. The only one who has all the answers to your fears, your life. You are the only one who is able to know what your divinely chosen path is.

You can understand this only when you go within. When you go within, you are the one with the answers. You are the one with the way forward.

We would like those who have been given a diagnosis to sit quietly as we speak to you. These words carry light codes of healing to awaken the light within. As you are reading this book, you are healing your cells. You are remembering bit by bit everything you always knew about healing. Sense how it feels within your body when you listen to it, when you give your body the time, the love, and space to receive light. You are remembering that you are part of the unified field of light. There is no separation. Everything you may have been told about religion, about your body, about your mind, is another's perception of reality. You always knew, you truly always *knew* the answers, as your body was just talking to you.

It was your job to listen. Your job to hear what your cells were telling you. As you read this, you are receiving an activation of your cells. Your DNA is lighting up, and you are remembering more of who you truly are. More of who you chose to be in this time, in this experience. You are a being of infinite light and love. There is nothing that you cannot have or be.

You were meant to experience this joy and bliss, and now it is yours to feel. It's yours to hear, yours to experience. Never doubt that you are loved, never doubt that you are walking this path on your own, and never doubt that you chose to be here and have this beautiful human form to let you know when you had forgotten.

7

Manifesting and Abundance

GUIDES: So let us talk to you about Mother Earth. You might see the earth as plants, trees, ground, and the soil. But we see so much more. We see a golden earth that is birthing. You might see the earthquakes, volcanoes, fires, and disasters, but we see evolvement, we see healing, and we see more light coming to this planet than ever before. As you expand your light, you are healing Mother Earth, you are healing the emergence of the golden earth. Do not listen to the fear; listen to your heart, to your inner knowing, to your universal guidance.

We are here to guide you. As this channel is writing these words, she sometimes doubts herself, but she knows she is always guided— that is her level of trust. She doesn't listen to the news or fear from people's mouths; she listens to her heart. We wish for you to listen to your heart, to listen to that part of you that knows no bounds, that knows the answers. The media play a huge part in trying to influence you. You can be influenced if you allow it, but by reading these words, you can be sure that you were guided to listen. Your soul guided you to hear these words because you know so deeply that this was perfect: this was the time to read them, the time to know. It was your time to awaken to the light within your beautiful heart.

By listening to your inner guidance, you are able to wake up those parts of you held deep within the cellular structure: the DNA, the cells, and therefore the light. With this awakening, you are able to sparkle and shine your light so much more brightly than you could ever imagine, with so much more ease and grace and so much more clearly to reflect the light—more than you have ever seen before.

You will never really know how much love we have for you until you walk with us again. However, remember the first time you fell in love, the first time you held a baby animal or a child, and that will give you a tenth of how loved you really are. It is your journey to remember this feeling.

Manifesting

What is manifesting? The word "manifestation" means the act of creating something or turning something from a thought or idea into a reality. In psychology, "manifestation" generally means using our thoughts, feelings, and beliefs to bring something to our physical reality. As you read the words following, you will see it's all about feelings and frequency.

Manifesting in human form is how you can see how much light you are holding. What you are manifesting is happening as a moment-by-moment experience. It is you creating your level of light. You have the power to bring more light into your field. Ask to be shown; ask your soul what you need to heal. Ask, keep asking, and keep loving *you*. The key is to listen and keep finding ways to love yourself.

This life was never about sacrificing yourself for others. It was never about treating yourself badly. It was never about feeling less than another. When you awaken to the light within, you are able to remember who you truly are and what you chose to do here. The mission you chose becomes clearer and clearer as the days move on.

Moment by moment, you become the reflection of your light. As your light gets brighter, your life appears happier and brighter.

We see so many of you giving your power away to others. We see the sadness and the dimming of your light ... we see you struggle with this. We are here to help guide you to your soul's love, that part of you that knows no bounds. That part of you that is perfect—just perfect. It's the part of you that never judges you, the part of you that sees the incredible light you are in the world.

If you would like to manifest something, manifest from a place of love, peace, and excitement for your mission, your service to humanity. As you focus your intention to manifesting from peace and love, watch how you see your life transform and change. Incredible souls, opportunities, abundance, and love all show up.

Expansion

Expansion is found with the awakening of the light within your heart. The channel has experienced great expansion and joy in her life since finding the light within, fully living her divinity and chosen life path. Your answer to true expansion, abundance, and joy is found in your light within your heart. As your heart heals, your light expands, and this reflects your life.

Abundance and Money

This is a subject we know you all love to have fun with. We also know that this subject brings so much fear to you, as all you really focus on is money. On your human plane of existence, this is one thing that many of you struggle with. We smile as we write these words, as you are missing what money really is.

Money is the vibration of love, the vibration of remembering who you are. That part of you that knows no bounds. Money, my dear child, is a reflection of you, the love you feel for yourself; the reflection of our love for you is constant. Look at your bank account and see how much you truly love yourself. You will find the answer there. We know that this seems unfair, and some may say cruel, but you were meant to understand money as a vibration, as love. You were meant to understand money as part of the unified field of consciousness, as part of you.

So we say the reason your bank account is not overflowing with money is that you have some dust in your field—just a tiny bit of dust that needs to be cleaned. Use our feather duster to clear these bits of debris and dust—it allows you to feel that you are clear, and therefore you will see so much difference in your bank account.

Surrender to us, as we are always guiding you.

If you remember that you are part of everything, that you are that which you project to the world, then you know that you are the money you have. So your projection of light reflects your projection of money.

You decided to remember that when you are in lack, you are in lack of light. That does not mean you are not a loving being, just that you are lacking the love of yourself and therefore alignment to your mission. Money is a great way of showing you that you are in alignment with mission or out of alignment with mission. Mission is pure love and freedom to serve. (See Chapter 10 for more on the soul's mission.)

If you are in pure alignment with mission, you will have freedom. In your earthly plane, that does not mean lack or abundance. It depends totally on what you chose to experience—what parts of your soul you wanted to expand. For some, it might be relationships, and then with love and equal relationship comes more freedom and money.

You may be loving your mission but not have enough money to live. So that would tell you that something you were meant to experience regarding your mission is not present. When this aspect is present, the money or freedom will flow. Remember that with more freedom, you can be of more service.

We would like to help you. Place your hands on your heart, close your eyes, and breathe. Ask your soul what your soul would like to experience to help you align more fully to your mission. If you do not receive a clear answer, then just trust that the answer will come. Watch out for signs, a person, place, or object. Just watch and acknowledge, and when the sign comes, thank yourself.

Gratitude is equal to loving yourself. We would like to talk to you about gratitude and the vibration of being grateful.

If you can tap into how it feels, then you are in the frequency of co-creating with the universe. If you can experience how it feels when you looking at a beautiful scene, a butterfly, a baby animal, a newborn child, the sea, the sky, then when you connect with that feeling, you are connecting with love, which is the same vibration as gratitude.

So we would ask you to write a list of things to be grateful for, and then when you are done, write another list of things to be grateful for towards yourself. Keep writing until you can write no more. Place this list in front of you, put your hand on this list, and ask for pure love to be poured into the list; this love will be poured into you. Feel this love as you drift off to sleep or start your day.

Freedom

This leads us to talk about freedom. Essentially, money gives you freedom. It allows you to serve in a way which is aligned to the divine flow of life. It allows you to be present to abundance and love. Money allows opportunity to feel expansive, to share your love in a broader way. You were never meant not to receive money, you were never meant not to receive love, and you were never meant not to be in complete, absolute freedom.

Freedom from chains was your birthright. You chose this unified field to experience pure freedom within this human form.

8

The Unified Field of Light and Our Emotions

The unified field is what you all are part of. You are connected with this field of light. There is no separation, there is no part of you that is not free, no part of you that is not abundant in thought, no part of you that is limited. There is not one part of you that is not connected together with the unified field.

So why is it that you feel separated from each other? Why is it that you feel that we are different and disconnected? Why is it that you choose to fill spaces or voids with things substances, people outside of ourselves to feel connected?

If you remember that you are never separated, never disconnected and never alone, you will never feel that you need to look outside of yourself to find the feeling of connection. You would not feel the need to search for the peace as you would know that the peace was within at all times, never outside of you.

Relationships were never created to fill a space, relationships were created to show us that you are a mirror to each other. To see which parts of yourself that you need to love more, which parts of you that you need to give compassion to and understanding? To love one another without judgement.

When you forgive yourself you are able to forgive others. You are able to see that we are all one light and part of the unified field. The unified field is all you need to remember. To remember that we are all one light, that we are all connected and there is no separation. When you remember that you can see that you attract those around you that reflect that part of you that is whole always was whole you were never broken or needing fixing. The soul part of you.

We are completely free to live this light that we chose to shine in this lifetime. To remember that as we shine our light we can show others that they can shine theirs too.

So how do we remember? When we sit quietly with our hands on our heart loving every cell of our body this is a good start. When we remember that we are never on our own, that we walk this plane of existence with our guides, helpers, loved ones, we know that we can remember that ease and grace that we are truly blessed to have within.

This human form was always supposed to experience joy and some may say peace on earth as it is in heaven. We would like to say it is all about loving who you are. Loving that part of you that exists in this unified field. Remembering that there is no separation. With this insight and remembering we can see that is it important to remind you that you are the ones that chose to come at this time to spread your light and create the golden earth, the new earth. This earth has been being created throughout time so it is not new. It is now just with your awakening, it was be realised in this timeline. It has always been there to be felt experienced and enjoyed, you just forgot.

You forgot when you were born. You chose it this way, there is no mistake. So we would say to you when you question why would I forget. Why wouldn't you?

Imagine if you remembered it all there would be no reason to be here in this human form. No reason to be here, no reason to feel emotion.

Let us talk to you about emotion.

Experiencing emotion was your way of finding the answers of how much love you felt for yourself. How much light you hold in your unified field. How much joy you are experiencing.

So you might say, "Why do I want to experience pain sadness, fear and not just only joy and happiness?"

We would say that if you alone experienced only joy, how would you know that you were out of the love vibration? How would you know that you were not living your divine path, the path you chose this time? How would you know? So you decided to experience this human form to experiment with your soul's consciousness. To feel and know and to remember that love is the only way you can heal, feel joy, and experience bliss.

This truly was what you chose. We know that it seems a hard path sometimes, and when you see so many suffering in their lives, you wish you could help them and heal them. It is not your job to heal anyone else. It's your job to heal yourself and remember who you are and why you are here. It never was your job to do another's journey. In fact, when you try to do this, you are actually preventing them from moving towards the path of divinity.

The path of divinity is yours to live. With divinity comes freedom within, freedom to choose the things, the people, and the life you want to manifest, and not just by default. You truly chose to create within the unified field of expansion. The way you can help those who have not remembered is to be the expression of compassion and love and truly know that they are guided too, that it is their choice to listen to their guidance. It's their choice to love themselves, their choice to love their bodies, and their choice to listen to the messages within.

How do we remember, you ask? You look at your outside reflection, your outside world. This is your knowing. You can see that there are things, people, places that are in the joy vibration, and there are things that are not. The things that are not, are not of the vibration of love. That doesn't mean that these people are not kind or loving; it just means that they are not reflecting the essence of true mission.

Everyone has come with their own unique reason for being here, their own unique reason to serve and spread their light. Yours will be different to another's. There is no judgement with this; only compassion and love. You have come to expand the light of the golden earth, and how you do that is in your own special way. You may be one who tends the earth and plants, like a gardener. You may be one who sails the sea, or you may be one who cares for children and animals. You may be one who cares for older members of the earth or builds homes to live in.

It matters not to us: all we see is pure love and light within you. We see only a unified field. We can watch and see this expand as you are loving to yourself and others. We are in complete love of you and your mission, and we are here to guide you and support you. You are never on your own.

You never designed it so as to do this journey alone. You chose to be given this guidance system, the body, as we have spoken about it, the mind with emotions and thoughts, and of course your inner guidance—your GPS for the soul.

Finding the peace within is your key. Daily practice of quietness is essential to your remembering. Within this book, you are finding many ways to connect with that pure guidance within. The processes in Part Three are essential to add to your daily healing work and daily practice.

The reality that you feel you live in is of your own making. It is real to you; however, it is not truly real. It is a reflection of your beliefs and how much love and light you hold in the unified field and therefore your field of light.

As you look around, you may see suffering, fear, wars, and destruction. We would like to invite you to consider that your emotions and reaction to these outside world events will be your key to seeing how much inner peace and light you hold within. So we would say, how do you feel about what you hear? How do you feel about what you see in front of you? How do you feel about the world that presents itself to you?

Whatever your answer, we are in joy. Whatever you feel, we are in gratitude for you. Whatever you see, we love you more than words can say. We are your guiding light within, and there is nothing that will ever stop that. You can talk to us and hear us by just sitting quietly for a few minutes a day. You do not need to sit for hours to connect; we are always here with you, guiding you.

Who are we, you ask? This channel would say we are your chosen team. You are we, we are you. We chose to be with you at this time, and we chose to never leave your side. Blessed one, we love you dearly.

When you sit quietly every day, we will guide you in ways you never thought were possible. We will tell you where your light is dusty. We will tell you how to be in the divine flow of abundance and step more fully into your mission. We will guide you every step of the way. You will not doubt; you will trust us as we love and trust you.

Trust is such a difficult one for you. When you awaken the light within, you are able to hear us more clearly, to hear your body and your divine mission.

Your lack of trust has been created from many times before. You are just light, you are just love—nothing more. There have been many past lifetimes that you have not remembered, and this is what is held in your field. It is an imprint that is held in your unified field of light. (We will revisit the topic of trust in Chapter 9.)

As you read this, feel into our words; feel into what is being healed in your heart field. What are you holding on to that you no longer need? Breathe, and ask for it to be healed.

What old beliefs are you choosing to keep in your field? You truly are love; you truly are light. There is never a need to hold anything that is not this vibration. It is just your beliefs that are held that create the outside world and the reflection within.

As you look at your light, just for a moment, we wish for you to see those interruptions in your field. Look at them, acknowledge them, love them, and release them. Forgive those parts of you that forgot that you were light and love. Forgive those parts of you that knew so much more but didn't remember. Forgive yourself for not seeing before. For not understanding, not listening. Forgive yourself as you perfect in our eyes, perfect in your light; create this golden earth with us by your side.

9

Parents and Choosing

Especially if you have had a seemingly hard life, with poverty, lack, or even abuse, you are probably wondering, *Why would I choose the parents I have?* Your soul has chosen to expand your own consciousness and that of your parents and family. As we have said before, you have had many lives before and many of them would have been with these parents, just playing out different roles.

You chose your parents, and they chose you, to experience unconditional love. You may say, "But why would I choose these parents, that abuse, that loneliness, that fear?" We ask you to remember that you chose them to understand unconditional love of yourself. You chose them to experience forgiveness. You chose them to know that one day you would remember—you would remember who you were. You would remember that you are a soul having a human experience, so that you would find a place within your heart to forgive them and to give them compassion.

In Chapter 22, you will find a process called Cutting the Ties that Bind with Forgiveness, which will help you to heal the relationships in your life without judgement and fear. As you forgive them, you are also forgiving yourself, as there is no separation in the unified field; we are all one. This process is a beautiful way of healing yourself though another and a way of seeing that only love exists. When you can see that there is only love and that your parents gave life to you for love, you can forgive on a deep level because you chose it with them.

As you speak the words from unconditional love, you feel the release in your heart. Even if your parent has passed, you can still heal this, and as you do, they evolve too. You are helping them to heal within the unified field and bring more love and light to this experience.

Contracts

GUIDES: We wish to talk to you about soul contracts. These are decisions or contracts that you chose to bring in, to hold for others within the unified field of light. Some examples of contracts are fear, loss, shame, and guilt. By choosing to hold these contracts, you have chosen to help others to bring more light. You are one that has chosen to step forward to be a guiding light for others. You are very special.

Contracts are held in the vibrational field and will play out in your life to show you the experience. You needed to experience this feeling, and in some cases discomfort, so that you could attract those who needed to heal. Now that you recognise the patterns in your life, you can see where the contracts have been held. You can release these contracts now and no longer need to hold them. It is your free will to let them go.

Ask to be shown any contracts that you may hold. Put your hands on your heart and breathe. As you breathe, ask, "Show me the contracts I no longer need to hold." Listen or feel where they may be held and ask for them to be released, keeping all the learning and love that you expanded from holding this vibration.

We have much love and gratitude for those who chose to hold these contracts and honour your decision with great love.

Clearing Ceremony to heal contracts. *Today I choose to rescind this contract that I chose from time before time to hold for the collective. I choose to set myself free from holding this contract. I choose to forgive myself as I set myself free of all lifetimes, including this one, that negatively were affected by holding this contract. I release this contract from a place of unconditional love.*

Judgement of Others

We know that you are sharing this world together, and we know that each one of you is a reflection of the light. This is something that you find hard to remember, and so the judgement of another comes into play.

Remember, dear soul, that as you judge another, you are judging yourself. As you judge another, you are looking at yourself. Just pause for a moment to consider this. Remembering this allows you to see what parts of your human experience you are judging. Then be kind to yourself; understand yourself. Ask what part of you needs compassion and understanding. Find one of the processes to help you to heal this part and bring more love and light into your heart.

Remember, you are your own inner healer. You can heal yourself. The Emotional Wall process in Chapter 19 works really well for situation and emotions like these. Try it out.

10

The Soul's Mission

Mission is different to purpose. You all have the same purpose: to remember who you are, to remember that you are pure love and with this you bring your love and light to the planet. Most important of all to remember that you can heal yourself. Mission, however, is different for everyone. It was something that you chose to experience with this physical body. It is unique to you and your journey of expansion.

No two missions are the same. Yours is perfect for you. No mission is better than another's. Each has the purpose of bringing more light to the unified field, but this is done in your own special way. There are signposts along the way, and you cannot do it wrong.

You are following your path beautifully, meeting the people you need to meet, healing those parts you chose to heal, learning to love yourself more every day while living your mission. This is the true joy of being human—the joy of remembering that you are a soul having a human experience.

Intention

Intention is your soul guiding you. When you are listening to your soul, you are guided to set intentions for your journey. Isn't that a beautiful way of listening?

What are you feeling you would like to focus on? How does it feel when you think about focusing on it? What resistance do you have? What emotion is held in that resistance? That is your key to releasing any energy that you are holding to stop you carrying out your soul's guidance.

- Sit quietly with your hands on your heart and ask for the perfect intention for your life.
- Then sense how it feels.
- Ask for the releasing of any emotion that comes up.
- Write down your intentions, if you choose, and ask for any emotions that do not feel good to be released with each one.
- Bring sparking light into your body and breathe.

You have the power to heal yourself. If you are excited by something, then it's for you. If you feel tired by it, it's probably not the perfect alignment for you. Do the exercise and see how you feel about the intention. If you feel fear about your intention, it might be that you needed to release fear or another unwanted emotion before feeling excited about your intention. Remember, you have lived many lives before and can hold old fears from those times.

Accidents

There are no mistakes, nothing is by accident, and no "accident" is an accident. Your vibrational light field is a reflection of your beliefs, your shocks, and your traumas. You are reflecting like a mirror out to the world, and the world is reflecting back to you.

Think of the last time you had an accident. What do you feel was the message your body was showing you? What were you experiencing in your life at that time? What do you feel you learnt from this? Where and what did you heal?

Many times, if you cannot hear your soul, your soul will create an experience to stop you or slow you so that you can listen. Even as you are reading this, if such an experience has happened, place your hands on your heart, connect with your heart, breathe, and ask your soul, What do I need to know?

Listen to our guidance. If you feel you need to write down what your soul tells you and come back to it, all is well. You have sent the intention that you are choosing to listen to your soul's guidance, and we are listening. It is your job to ask and it is given.

Cleansing Your Auric Field

The auric field is the energy field around you. Mediums can see this clairvoyantly; however, most people can't. It is the light frequency around you that attracts a match of what you are putting out to the universe. It holds the beliefs, thoughts, emotions, and energy of you.

You can cleanse your auric field with rainbow light.

- Imagine seeing a waterfall of light washing over you. You are remembering that you can visualise and create whatever you desire. You are your own inner healer with everything within you.
- Imagine standing under a waterfall. Wash away all debris from your field; wash away your unwanted emotions and beliefs in this waterfall of light.
- Imagine sitting with your feet in the water, splashing in a clear pool of water. Know that as you do this, you are clearing your field with just the intention of cleansing your light field; you are asking, and it is given.

Using visualisation allows you to let go, allows your soul to talk to you and allows you to listen more deeply to your mission.

Connecting with Your Soul's Mission

Here is an easy process to access information about your own soul's mission and spread your light of intention.

1. Place your hands on your heart, close your eyes, and breathe. Imagine a beautiful golden-pink sparkling light filling your heart. See it as a ball of light, then send this ball of light up to the universe and out to the world and then back to you. This action allows you to send your love out to everyone who needs to connect with you, and to bring it back. This visualisation hands over the need to think about how to reach more people as it is done. We would ask you to do this on a daily basis and watch what happens.

2. Each day, place your hands on your heart, close your eyes, and ask your soul, "What do I need to know?" Write this down and create a journal of insight. Your soul knows exactly what you need to align to your mission.

3. Drink lots of water, and ask which foods are perfect for your vibration. You will soon see that there are particular foods and drinks that stop being appealing to you. As you hold more light in your field, you choose light-reflecting foods. Another way of helping this process is to bless your food and drink with light. This light is the light of love and the unified light field. It transmutes any energy of pain and darkness.

What we mean by pain is the pain and shock that an animal may have experienced before passing. Some animals are prepared, but some are not, and this shock is held in the body as a vibration. You can heal this by pouring love, gratitude, and light into the food.

Then as you eat this, you are eating pure light and love, and you will absorb the nutrients perfect for your physical body.

Choice is your soul guiding you. Make no decisions based on another's, as it is theirs, not yours. When making a decision about food choices, place your hands on your heart, close your eyes, breathe, and ask, "Is this in alignment with my soul's mission?" If the answer is yes, then go ahead; if not, then listen for a more aligned choice. As you start to do this on a daily basis, you will develop such an inner knowing that you will never question your guidance again. You will just know.

More on the Unified Field

We would like to talk to you a little more about the unified field, this field of consciousness that you are part of. There is no separation from this field. You are an integral part of it. Your light with your frequency is a determining factor in the unified consciousness, and the journey within is the key to explaining that light. The journey within all your journeys within allows the unified field to expand.

So you may ask why that is important. Why do we need to expand the unified field? Well, this field of consciousness is responsible for the quality of your experience. We know that you want more freedom to explore your mission, and with this expansion of light, the freedom you wait for is contained within. Freedom is of course a state of mind; however, it is fundamentally a state of light or state of being.

So we invite you to listen now to your soul's guidance. We invite you to place your hands upon your heart and listen to your soul telling you how it is for you to expand your light field—your heart field, some will call it—and how you can step more fully into the ray of light that you always planned to be. Take time to do this now.

As we see you, you are perfect, and as you continue to see your light expand, day by day you will start to see yourself as perfect. That

51

there is no separation from you or us or them. That we are all part of this unified field of consciousness, exploring the aspect of being human.

Being human, we know, has many layers of consciousness. There are the lives you have come to heal, the ancestors' experiences, the thoughts that you have picked up along the way. This, my child, is all held in your light field. Your light field reflects out to you the exact mirror of your field of light. Oh, you say, but that person is unkind, that situation is not my fault; but we would say, you are responsible for what you attract into your experience. We say this with no judgement, just with love and understanding.

We walk with you every moment of your day, so you are never alone. Ask us for guidance all the time, and you have it; listen. There are many you will be guided to, just as you have been guided to read this book. This is in perfect alignment with your soul's guidance. It was time to hear these words, just as it will be time to experience whatever you are experiencing.

11

Love and the Guides

In this chapter, we will cover the concepts of how those in our lives, including animals, help us to heal; and how our guides are enabling us to trust ourselves more, and how they are with us every day.

Our Guides Are Showing Us the Way

GUIDES: Your soul is guiding you all the time; you just need to listen to it. Each time you listen, you are becoming more in tune with that part of you that has all your answers, that part of you that knows no bounds. There are others that help and support you too. You are blessed with other beings of light. These beings are not separate from you but are all part of the unified field. Essentially, we are you, and you are we. In fact, we are all one.

We are here to guide you and show you the way. You were guided to read this book, and you were guided to listen. Love yourself for listening; love yourself for showing up and not giving up. Love yourself as we love you.

We have travelled with you from the light to the light. We know that you feel you need to know our names, but we are beings from the light just as you are. We come with different vibrational fields to assist you in this time. Some have requested us to work with certain aspects of you at this time, and others with different aspects. Connect with us now. Know that we come from pure love for you to you—to help you.

Ask us anything you need. Ask now as you place your hands on your heart, breathe, and listen. We will show you the next part of your soul's divine plan. We will help you to align with your mission and the people you chose to meet. We will guide you to deeply care and love yourself. We will guide you to heal. Know that we will guide you; we always have and always will.

Healing comes from within; however, with our guidance we will help you pinpoint the exact belief that you are holding which is dimming your light. As you tell us your deepest desires, we will tell you how to heal to align to them.

Trust

We now wish to talk to you about trust.

When you are in divine guidance of your soul's mission, you feel the sense of trust throughout your whole being. You know that you are never on your own, you are always guided, and you are provided for at all times. You are loved.

This is pure trust. Trust that you are a being of light. Trust that you are loved; trust that we are here to support you and hold your hand. We are here to walk across your mountains, to walk in the waters, to walk in the sand. Wherever you travel, walk, feel, we are there with you.

When you sleep, we are with you. You are connected to us as we are connected to you. You meet with us, you meet with your loved ones and the souls you journey with, and you raise more healing light to the earth. You may not remember these journeys, these meetings, these moments. But your soul knows the journey you have been on.

If you ask before you go to sleep to travel with us, to meet with us, to remember something of your mission, we will show you. We will imprint this memory for you so that you will be guided to heal or experience this.

If you wish to meet with another soul, do this from a place of pure love, to connect with them on a soul level, to remember your soul contracts together.

Fear and False Prophets

At this time, there are many you will call false prophets. Do not fear those who are not truthful. You have your own unique guidance system, your soul. Ask, "Is this person, is this place, is this job, is this home in perfect alignment with my mission?" Feel the answer; feel the feeling you have when you think about it. Feel where you hold this is in your body. Does it feel good, loving, and clear? Does it feel heavy, dark, and confusing? These are ways that you can be guided to the perfect alignment for your soul's mission. You have all the answers within.

Do not judge yourself for attracting situations, places, or things into your life that do not feel good. Just acknowledge that part of you needs more healing light, and let yourself be guided to the perfect process among those offered in this book to heal the child who felt the disconnection to their soul. Love them and watch your light shine more brightly. Thank that person in your heart or experience for coming into your life to show you your place to heal the light within.

You are awakening a brighter, clearer, more expansive light within you. Your life is changing as you read this; you are feeling more love for yourself, and you know you are deserving of this. You have your soul's guidance at all times. We are here to guide you too. You are never alone.

The healing codes within this book are transforming your light field. You are blessed now. Remember that you are a child of God, so beautiful, whole, and incredible. You are perfect to us; we see you as perfect. See yourself this way as you step more fully into your mission. Your light expands as your light shines brighter and brighter. We see your light as so beautiful—not the way you see it. We see all those you touch with your light. There is nothing wrong with you.

Those who tell you that you are broken, that you are not whole, are not seeing what we see. When you tell yourself that you are not good enough, you create a frequency of that within your body. We only see that you are pure light and energy. When you feel you are ugly, we see you as beautiful. When you feel you can't be in this world anymore, we send you strength. You are never on your own.

Never look outside yourself for love. You are pure love. You hold the vibration of love. When you awaken to the light within, you remember that you are pure love, that you need no one to confirm this within you. You are in trust that you are here because you chose to be here. You know that you are divinely guided. If you see that you are seeking another to tell you that you are love, go within. If you are in a relationship with someone that feels like need, you feel the fear, you will feel doubt, and you will feel unlovable. Take your time to heal the parts of you that felt unlovable, that forgot you were never alone. Remember that you are never separated; we are all one—one unified field of existence sharing this world.

Look at your relationship and feel. "Is this loving me? Is this loving me? Is this loving me? Is this nearer to my mission?" These are all questions that you can ask your inner knowing, your soul that part of you, that has all the answers. Use the Cutting Ties process in Chapter 22 to heal your relationship. This is done with pure love and forgiveness; watch how it transforms. If it is meant, it will blossom; if it is complete, it will change and end. There is a vibrational match which is better for you. You are pure love, and you deserve to be with someone who loves themselves equally. Heal the mirror of the reflection that is not feeling loved.

You know deep inside that you can heal yourself. You have the power to heal yourself. We will guide you to awaken the light within your heart.

Decisions that are made from the light in your heart are always in alignment with your soul's mission. Decisions that are made from your mind are sometimes clouded by fear. When we remember times before when we had to make decisions that scared us, they are usually from other lifetimes and our ancestors and are just being triggered in this life. This "now" moment is made up of all the other now moments that your soul has known.

Ancestors and Times Before

The vibrational field that you bring in is the one you chose to experience as your physical body or vehicle to carry your soul. Many lifetimes before, you had decided that you would bring aspects of yourself to heal in this lifetime. This was to help the others who were not able.

You are here at a very special time, a time of great transformation. We are honoured that you chose to heal these past timelines of your ancestors who walked before you. As you connect with your ancestors, listen to their wish.

- Place your hands on your heart and breathe.
- Listen to what you brought in to heal this time. Listen. Feel it and love that part of you that chose to bring it in. Know that you can heal it for you and your ancestors now. It is done.
- Write a list of what you are being told.
- Connect with your heart, and ask for your healing sound to vibrate through you to heal this ancestral belief. You can use your healing sound to fine-tune your vibration to healing your light field. Take a breath and allow the sound to be released.

- Ask for the specific thing to be healed. Then connect with your heart and listen for the sound to heal.
- Check in: is this healed? Then move on if it has been. If not, ask for another sound to heal it. You have your own healing sound that is part of you.

You always knew that you could heal yourself. You just forgot that you had everything within you.

You can use this process every day to bring more light into your field.

Relationships

People leave or stay with us when our vibration is a reflection of that. People never leave or stay in our lives unless we are that direct reflection. You cannot keep someone or control someone unless they are of that attraction and reflection. For example; anger, fear, mistrust and guilt.

Think back to times when relationships have ended. We know that this was painful for you at the time. But when you look back now, you can see that your vibration, your energy, was not a match anymore for that experience. It makes human sense now, doesn't it?

If you are struggling with a "breakup", as you would call it on your human plane, then we ask you to place your hands on your heart now, breathe, and feel into the experience. Release those tears; release the pain and suffering. Ask us to help you release now.

The time has come to heal the imprints of these lives that came before these doubts in your light, these doubts in how loved you are by us. Let go; let go and allow a flooding of our love to fill your heart, to fill you so deeply that you will never question your worth. You will attract now a new vibration. A new energy will be a match. All is well; all is perfect for you.

Your only job is to heal you. Ask for our help to find the right person or process experience to help you to release this energy held in your field. We love you so much, and we always will.

Walk in Mother Earth's nature. Be immersed in the sea, in the park, in the woods. Feel the energy of the elementals taking care of you and Mother Earth. Feel the support of Mother from the earth. You are a divine human, and you have a divine mission for being here at this time.

Animals

When you start to see this incredible soul's journey ahead of you, you are able to see the beauty in the world. You are able to see the love in animals, those pets that choose you to be part of their experience, the beautiful souls that came to open our hearts to love. If you have a pet, be aware of how it feels when the pet is with you. Whether it is a bird, lizard, cat, dog, horse, whatever, like you, it has a soul's mission here to support you and help you return to love. As you look into a pet's eyes, you know you can feel unconditional love. They want nothing back from you except that you love, feed, and keep them safe.

After you have read these words, each time you see an animal from now on, we wish for you to connect with what its soul is trying to help you with. Connect with the soul of each animal that is divinely guided to journey with you, and listen to what your journey is together.

When an animal passes, you have an opportunity to heal deep grief from many times before. You have that opportunity to heal that part of you that could not cry, could not feel that emotion of sadness—that part of your heart that was closed. Thank that animal for allowing you to heal.

Animals heal you on a deep level. You will see many animals with psychical illnesses. This illness is the absorption of your emotions. Do not feel bad as you read this; just know that your animal chose to heal you and chose to journey with you. Just love is shown to you by your animal. Shower your pets with love and gratitude for their presence. Thank them for choosing you to care for them as they chose to care equally for you.

When an animal leaves us—whether by accident, sudden death, being lost—it is helping us to heal those parts of us that could not heal before.

Susan's Guides and Helpers

This channel has many guides who work with her. We wish to introduce a few of the main ones who assist her on her mission.

Pleiadian Collective

We are the ninth-dimension Pleiadian collective, and we are here to guide you and support you in listening to what your soul needs. We are very pleased to assist you.

We channel light codes to heal the vibration of resentment and anger that is held in the heart. We also balance the light and love held in the heart to allow more light to flood in. Through this channel we do this by sound and light codes. You may have heard this called the language of light.

We are here to guide you. Ask us to do so.

You may experience us as silvery-blue light in colour and tall in presence.

Mother Mary

I came to work with this channel to heal the suffering child within you, the child within that cannot feel safe or loved. I do this by singing sounds and coming close to you, holding your baby or child self as your mother.

I am here to love and guide you and release your suffering. Please ask, as I am never far away.

Jeshua or Jesus

I work with this channel to help you to trust and surrender to receiving love. Now is the time to remember who you are as a child of God and that it is time to surrender to trust. As you surrender to trusting that all is well and that you are always guided and looked after, your life will open to new levels of love.

Love is all there truly is in this world. You are a being of love, pure love, pure energy. It is for you to remember that you are truly blessed with everything you need to carry out your mission here. You do not need to know exactly where you are going, only to trust your heart and follow your soul's guidance.

Through this channel, I am here to remind you that you are loved. Ask me to help and support you in your time of need.

Arcturians

We are the Arcturians, and we work with this channel to clear old stories held in your field from the past. We clear these with light language and tones.

You will also experience the Arcturian Council if your mission is to be a teacher in this world. You receive messages from us.

This channel sees us as golden in our energy imprint. This is because of the high frequency we hold.

Melchizedek

I am the overseer of the universe and all beings of the light. I come with activations to raise more light to guide you on your mission. I hold my book of codes for you to help you and stand by your side. I see exactly what you need to assist you on your soul's mission. You receive activations of pure love, and you will feel a sense of peace and knowing.

Ask for my healing activations to assist you on your mission. I am also present in all of this channel's remote healing Galactic Crystal Chambers.

Feminine Source

This aspect of Source is a high frequency tone aligning you to the divine feminine. This alignment allows you to receive a pouring of love into your field of light though your crown and aligns you more easily to receiving your birthright of receiving pure abundance. This is a combination of the goddess energy and angelic frequency.

Masculine Source

This comes in a very low vibrational tone releasing the lower vibrations of guilt, shame, fear, shock, and any attachments that may be present. This energy is a combination of councils of light working together to release unwanted darkness and dust from your field of light.

Ashtar

I am Ashtar of the Galactic Command, a higher consciousness and part of the Council of Light.

I stand with this channel as her guide at this time. She is here to guide and help others navigate their souls' missions.

With all these beautiful beings of light from Source, ask and it is given. Be specific in what you would like to heal.

Ask your guides, and even if you don't know who they are, ask them to heal specific things for you. For example, say, "I feel fear of completing my mission" instead of "I feel fear," which is too general. Be specific and say something such as "I feel fear of success," or of failure or being seen.

12

"We Love You"

GUIDES: You are here to experience two aspects of yourself: the divine feminine, and the divine masculine.

As you connect with the divine feminine, you are in receiving mode, as you might call it. As you heal your relationships to your own mother, you are healing your relationship to Mother Earth and your relationship to being human. You are perfect in your light. You are ready for this. Heal your relationship to Mother. (For a process, go to Chapter 22, "Cutting the Ties that Bind with Forgiveness".)

Now it is time to heal your relationship to Father. The divine masculine gives you the focus for how you are going to serve and stand in your mission. Your connection to your soul's divine mission is held here—your connection to God/Source. Do the same Cutting the Ties healing process with Father now.

With both of these relationships healed, we can see your light shine more brightly. We can see that there is a balance in your field. You will see now that you have a softer experience in your life. You will be able to receive gifts from the unified field, gifts of love and money, gifts to assist you on your mission. The freedom you desire, which is your birthright, will be with you now. Place your hands on your heart, and listen to us as we will guide you through your breath.

Your breath holds the space to feel that peace that you have within. Your breath allows you to listen; your breath allows a deeper connection to the unified field of light.

We wish to remind you that you are perfect. Nothing is wrong with you. You are a beautiful being of light having a human experience.

You may have heard the words *Peace on Earth as it is in Heaven*. That is exactly how it is. We will explain.

On a level of consciousness, you are always in peace and pure connection to your soul. On a human level, you are remembering. When you awaken the light within your heart, you are able to find that true peace once again—the peace that you had forgotten.

Whilst living this human experience, you will have many experiences when you will feel the lack of peace. We know this, and we ask you at these times to place your hands on your heart and ask for your soul's peace. Your soul's guidance and you will be found. When we say "found", we mean your soul and the human part of you will be unified. As this takes place, you connect with your inner knowing of your divine mission.

Your divine mission is to spread the light in your own unique way. You are unique in your human form, and your chosen mission is unique to you.

We see so much competition on the earth at this time, and we would ask you to connect with your soul at times of confusion and fear and feel the inner knowing that you are perfect as you are, your mission is unique, and your gift of love is yours to share. When you remember this, and when you awaken the light within, you are truly in a space of divine guidance of your soul.

We come to you through these words to hold you, love you, and feel that inner safety and trust that we know you so desire. We are here to tell you that we are always here with you. There is never a need to exist in the fear of the unknown, as there is no unknown. Your soul knows everything you need, and there is nothing to fear.

Your soul has no surprises; however, you are here to experience the joy of life as a human, so you will have plenty of what seem like surprises. Your field of light determines the level of joy in your life, the level of peace you experience. and the level love you feel within.

We love you.

Consciousness is the ability to project your guidance from your soul to your experience in the human form. Let us explain.

As you listen more clearly to the words and sounds, the signposts you are given, you will expand that consciousness into the unified field. Your field of light will be full of sparkles; your light will be seen from country to country, from planet to planet, from star system to star system. Your guidance will become stronger, and your inner knowing of your soul's mission will be so clear that you will instantly attract the people, places, and resources that you need to be that divine human on earth, to shine your light and help others to do the same.

It is your light that allows the unified field to expand, the great healing to take place that we have been supporting for you day by day since you chose to arrive again and have this human experience. We trust you, we love you, we are grateful that you chose this mission, and we are with you.

Peace will prevail in your world as more of you awaken to the light. Peace is the ultimate plan. With peace comes unity. This is the ultimate plan of the new golden earth, and you are part of this. You chose to bring peace though your own unique way. We honour you.

Now place your hands on your heart and breathe into your soul to hear those words of love and guidance. To hear who you truly are. To experience the love of your inner knowing that you are never on your own.

We see a golden earth; we see your earth as healing, with more light and peace. We see inside every one of you this beautiful light— even inside those in despair, darkness, and fear.

If as you read this you are feeling the despair of being human, we hold your heart in our hands and assist you in your healing journey.

There are many processes that we gave to this channel so that you can heal yourself. We will assist you in healing those parts of you that felt the fear of being abandoned, alone, and disconnected to Source, God, the universe, and ultimately to you.

When you awaken more light into your field, you will become lighter, your thoughts will become purer, your ability to hold more light will become easier for you, and your soul will be able to communicate with you in a deeper way. We are here to love you and support you. You have done no wrong in our eyes. You are a perfect being of light.

If you feel guilty for feelings you have about the wrongs you may have committed, we are here to tell you that there is no "Judgement Day", that there is no part of you that will be judged, and that the only judgement comes from you. We ask you to go on this healing journey with us and release the guilt, shame, and fear so that you can truly live a beautiful life. Your birthright was always freedom, to experience joy and abundance through remembering your mission, remembering who you are and remembering you are pure love.

Your mission was never to harm yourself or another; it was never to judge yourself or feel scared of the future. It was never your job to tell yourself that you are wrong. It was never your time to stay stuck.

It was never your job to stay in the dark; it was only your job to return to the light. To awaken the light within. That was always your mission.

We love you.

The only thing we really want you to know is this: when you awaken to the true light that you are, you are living your full potential and your desired dreams. We know that you are told you can think your dreams into reality, and to an extent this is true; however, we would rather help you to understand that it is your frequency of light not your dark that we see, and the more light you are able to hold, the more you will be able create in a specific way. Creating is from the extent of light you hold, and therefore love.

That does not mean that if you do not have pure abundance, you're not a loving person. It just means that you are not holding the pure potential of your light. The purest form of light is true abundance, which you may see as success. We like to refer to it as pure freedom. When you ask, it is given. It really is! It's just that you are asking depending on the light you hold, so you receive depending on the light you hold.

We know that you may have to read this again—well, at least this sentence, because this might say that everything you have been told has not been true. That is not so—it's just that we wish to remind you of something you already know and already knew before you came. It was your intention to remember that it was all about light and nothing else, and that the more light and love you hold, the more you are able to create your own life of freedom and truly live your purpose.

Living your purpose is just living in the light. Yes, we would say and agree that you all have chosen a specific reason; however, the same purpose is with you all. It is the same: living by the light. Awaken to the light that you truly are.

You are loved. You are blessed, and we are here with you.

Time in your existence is not really there. You have created a reality of time so that you may experience emotion. When you feel you do not have enough time, you will feel the pressure, the pain, and this will bring up old emotions from the past to be healed. This in itself is a good thing. This is why you created a timeline: so that you can work towards goals and intentions and heal whatever comes up in the way of completion. We would like to remind you that you truly can heal everything that comes up by just asking.

Place your hands on your heart, close your eyes, and breathe. Ask for the energy that you feel around an emotion to be released. Ask for all the timelines and lifetimes you have ever lived to be healed too. It is done.

Healing is simple. Healing is instant. No one can heal you. You are your own inner healer.

We ask you to be clear with your intention to heal … to be clear with exactly what you wish to heal.

Be clear of why. Then it is done.

We know that there are many healing modalities here on your earth, and this is just perfect at this time. They are there to assist you to access your own soul's knowing and to remember that you are ready to heal.

No healing modality is the holy grail. You are your own holy grail. So with this reminder, feel into how it is best for you to access your own soul's knowing and mission and to trust that the person, place, or process is just perfect for you at this time—that as your vibration changes, more light is held, and the modality and person will change too.

As people come into your life and come out of your life, know that all is perfect.

It is all about the light you hold. When you start to hold more light, then you will attract those with the same light into your world. It is because you are a mirror of the light. As the light reflects from you, it reflects out to the universe and right back at you. It is a great way for you to be able to see how much light you hold.

Let us talk now about the crystalline light field. This field is held in the body as light particles, and if you were to see them in human form, you would see them as diamonds or crystals sparkling. Each particle or diamond holds a vibrational frequency.

To raise the vibration of the particle, you can use your own healing sound. The channel writing this uses sound vibration from Source and the great central sun to resonate through these particles. Allow more light to reflect within you. This then joins the unified light field, creating a beautiful expansive beam going out to the universe and other galactic dimensions.

When you remember this, you will know that the more experiences you can have of pure love, the more you can hold the particles of light that reflect more freedom.

PART THREE

THE SPIRITUAL TOOLBOX

13

Assembling Your Spiritual Toolbox

For this part, I have chosen the most powerful processes and healing statements that I continue to use with my clients daily to help them to access the unseen, hidden, and blind spots that create blocks in success, relationships, and one's mission. These processes were seeded from working with veterans with PTSD; however, over the years they have evolved to help thousands of people heal aspects of themselves that continued to stop the flow in all areas of their lives.

The deep healing that is about to take place within you will change not only your perception of yourself but the vibrational frequency you hold. As your frequency changes, your life changes. The universe can align to you to bring you harmonious relationships, more money, a healthy body, and most of all the ability to live your true soul's mission.

Also included with the processes are testimonials from my clients, so that you can see that you too can heal. It is my intention that you live your best, most fulfilled life, and I am excited that you chose me to support you on your journey.

14

Muscle Testing

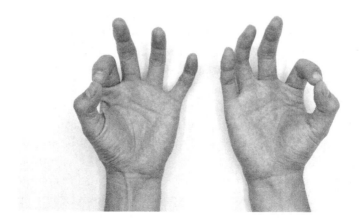

Muscle testing is used throughout the world to access what is truly held in one's field. It's a great way of knowing when you have cleared something. If you would like to practice it, here is a step-by-step guide.

To muscle test, make a circle with the thumb and ring finger of the hand you do not write with. Connect the thumb and index finger of your writing hand to form a link with that circle, as shown in the accompanying illustration. Now move apart your fingers on your writing hand to see whether the loop on the other hand stays closed or opens easily.

Test to see which your truth is. Does it stay open for a truth, or closed? Then you are ready to test some beliefs. Statements such as "I feel" or "I believe" are helpful to start with.

15

The Peace Scale

The Peace Scale will help you to move towards loving yourself. Awakening the light within brings you more peace than you can ever know, more peace than you can imagine. The guides hope that as you read these words, you can see that they are words of love. You can feel their love for you. It is boundless love; it has no end. It's far-reaching, and you are never on your own.

When you feel lack of peace, ask yourself, "What part of me is feeling this?" What part of you is feeling the lack of love of self? What part of you is feeling the lack of light? This is your key and answer to your lack of peace.

The Peace Scale ©

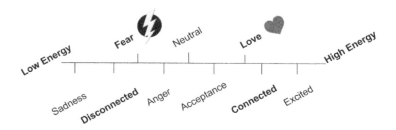

You always can access this peace, as you are that peace. Put your hands on your heart, close your eyes, and breathe. Imagine light coming into your heart centre, imagine a symbol of love coming into your heart field, imagine the light expanding out into every cell in your body, and see yourself as light. See yourself as a divine being here for a very special reason. You knew why, and you are remembering why now as you read this book you will have been drawn by your soul to read, as you are experiencing deep healing within.

16

Clearing Statement

Speak the clearing statement in any position that is comfortable for you. The eyes may be open or not. You may be sitting or lying down.

> Creator of all that is, it is commanded that you create a beautiful sacred space for me now. Please

clear, cancel, and delete any waywards, watchers, entities, attachments, anything that does not serve me now. Please do this on all four levels—mind, body, soul, and energy field—and resolve this on the history level across all timelines, lifetimes, past, present, future. Send to unconditional love/Source/ God. Thank you, thank you, thank you; it is done.

17

Earth Star*Soul Star Meditation

Earth Star*Soul Star

It is important to be connected to the Earth plane as well as the Universal and Multidimensional planes of existence. My guides gave me this process many years ago to allow us to feel connected in this human form as well as connected on a soul level. They tell me that many remember who they are but forget that they had agreed to be connected to Gaia or Mother Earth, especially if the experience with their own mother was not that supportive.

This meditation is a great process to allow you to ground and connect. Teach it to your children too, calling it the "Star in the ground, Star in the sky".

- Put your hands on your heart, breathing normally, and connect to your heart centre.
- Imagine a beautiful golden cord travelling from your feet into the ground. Watch as it goes deeper to find your Earth Star. Even if you can't see it, know and imagine it's there.
- Now imagine the golden cord travelling up to the top of your head and shooting up to the universe, where you will find your six-pointed golden Soul Star.
- Connect with the star, which contains all of the knowledge from all your lifetimes, where you remembered you were pure love and being of light. Bring it down to your heart.
- Expand that knowing and light throughout to the whole of your energy field, watching it sparkle.

Knowing you are connected to your Earth Star and Soul Star, you can develop a clearer connection to your guides helping you to feel safe in this world.

Use this process before each of the following processes. Also use the clearing statement in Chapter 16 to create a beautiful sacred space before doing any healing work or calling in your guides.

I use this process religiously every morning. It helps me stay grounded. I always use it for my clients during our sessions. I love it so much that I recently decided to teach this process during a workshop on Grounding. The feedback from my clients was phenomenal.

Client Testimonials

One of my clients, Roshney, went on to share this process with her own client.

Thank you for the session, Alina. It was wonderful. Spent the rest of the evening feeling like I'd taken the ultimate chill pill and I was feeling kind of stressed (teenage child blues) before it. I will definitely incorporate all I learned into my daily life.

Roshney

Roshney, I've had such an amazing sleep! I don't think I've slept this well since I was a young child.

Alina

18

Colour Energy Clearing

The Colour Energy Clearing process can be used on its own or with all of the other processes in this book to guide you on your healing journey. Children love this process, so you could try it with your child too. Get them to imagine using a magic wand to clear the colour with golden sparking light.

When we imagine or see colour during energy processes, it shows us that we are connecting to the emotion, energy block, or resistance.

When we can access the colour we are seeing, we can access the emotion we are holding. We can watch as it changes colour when we imagine golden sparkling light from our crown to our feet, clearing the emotion and the block, without needing to know where it came from.

- Start by doing the Earth Star*Soul Star process to ground and connect.
- Then focus in your body where you feel a particular emotion, such as fear.
- Give this emotion a colour, then imagine platinum light coming in from your crown energy and diffusing and releasing the colour of the emotion.
- Check in to see how you feel now about the situation. You may need to do it again, as the colour may have changed.
- If you still feel that you hold the emotion, try another process to release.

Here is a list of colours and my inspired interpretations of their significance. These colours may be used as well to help heal the blocks.

pink and gold sparkling	pure heart opening to seamless love
platinum sparkling	pure healing vibration (we can use this to transmute and align our connection to Source)
gold sparkling	beginning of freedom, and more light and energy in the field
magenta	higher communication
violet	cleansing light

These colours may be seen when there is a block or resistance in the field.

orange	empowerment/disempowerment
yellow	early childhood trauma
pink or green	heart, deep hurt, pain and rejection

blue	communication, not being heard or listened to
dark blue	another's way of communication (parents or ancestors) that you took on
turquoise	a need to save everyone the world (when I see this, that's usually what it means the person has had lives connected to Atlantis)
red	feeling unsafe, a lack of security in the world; can be frustration and anger
purple	healing grief towards your true spiritual purpose
white	fear; or when mixed with another colour, fear or a block associated to that particular colour
grey	old shock
black	old dense energy, past life, conception to birth

19

The Emotional Wall Process

The Emotional Wall was born from my work with war veterans diagnosed with PTSD, who had told their story so many times to psychologists and doctors that they were tired of repeating the trauma. The guides gave me this process to get to the root cause of the first time my client felt a sense of disconnection to Source/God/Universe due to trauma. We are never disconnected. However, when we experience trauma or perceptions of belief that are not true, such as words someone told us; events that lead us to be afraid of the world; or in fact anything that stops us from being the absolute best version of ourselves, then we have an instinct to protect our heart. An "emotional wall" is created within our heart.

This wall did serve a purpose at the time. The walls we create stay there until we are ready to shine more brightly. However, they can even stop us from living our mission. When we see that we are not able to manifest or attract what we need or desire, they show us our blocks to self-love. When we know we have walls, we can begin the process that will heal the child and disappear that wall.

Use the following process as many times as you feel you would like to, as there are many aspects of us that need healing.

- Think of the issue you are having at the moment, or just imagine fear as the wall.
- How high is your wall? Is it above your head, or below?
- What's over your wall? If you can't see anything, imagine what you would like to see.
- Imagine a child standing next to you. This is your inner child who needs healing and who has been outside you all your life, feeling fear.
- How old is the child standing next to you?
- How does that child feel about the wall in front of them?
- Can the child imagine what is on the other side of the wall?
- Put yourself in a golden ball of protective light, and your child in a another ball of light. Which colour light is the child standing in? You can check which emotion they are holding by the colour chart in Chapter 18, if you choose.
- Imagine three angels behind the child. One angel steps forward, holding a basket full of pure, sparkling stars. The angel holds out the basket for the child to choose one star at a time, starting with connection, unconditional love, empowerment, freedom, and happiness. You can also listen for many other emotions that the child may need—these are just the main ones in the basket. Another option is for the angel to give the child each one in turn. Look at the colour and once again connect with the emotion.
- How does your child feel now?

- What does the wall look like? Has it got smaller, or even disappeared?
- If the wall is still there, even partially, the angel now will give the child a magic wand and have them to whizz it all away. Make sure the magic wand clears all the remaining wall.
- What is in front of the child now? Has it changed? What do they see? Sometimes it's a playground, or a beautiful landscape, or a magical kingdom.
- Now it's time to integrate your inner child into your heart. This can be an emotional step, but it's an important part of the process, as we don't often give ourselves compassion and love. Turn to your child and say, "I will always love and accept you for who you are, whoever you choose to be in this world, and whomever you choose to share your life with. I am going to pop you in my heart where you will always feel safe, loved, and looked after, and we are going to have so much fun together, creating our dreams and living our mission."
- If the child is still stuck and not ready to integrate, you can also add with compassion, "I am so sorry you felt _____ [whatever emotion you feel drawn to say]." Keep doing this until the child is ready to come into your heart.
- What can you now see in front of you? Is it different? Brighter, maybe? More beautiful?
- Now it's time to walk forward into the scene. Say these words out loud, if possible: "As I walk forward, I let go of the past and move into the present which creates my future."
- Imagine the scene. You are standing in the picture, arms wide, embracing the new. Turn up the colours and sounds. Maybe there are animals, butterflies, birds, the sea, or trees. Imagine a dial being turned up. These are only a few ideas. Whatever you experience is perfect.
- Imagine how you feel in your heart in the scene. Breathe it in. Send the intention to the universe of the new imprinted version of you. Then bring that picture of you feeling free into your heart where you are sitting now.

- Watch how you start to manifest more easily in your life, that which you truly desire.

Client Testimonials

MT: The process I chose was the Emotional Wall. I want to heal the blockage I put on relationships. I have been single for many years, and I see me not opening up emotionally. You see, I never liked my father. He was cruel and sadistic, and the first seven years of my life was a living hell.

The emotional wall process allowed me to find my inner child. I found the process supportive, and it helped me feel secure by bringing my angels in. By following this process, I'm able to bring emotional walls down. It took more than one attempt, with me feeling sick, plus a pain in my gut that I felt has been released.

This process is amazing and helped me find the love of self. Finding your inner child and connecting to him and bringing him to your heart allows me to feel not so guarded. It's still early days, but I know this process worked for me, and I can do it again if I feel the need.

Clarissa Walker: I did The Emotional Wall process with Susan during an online workshop three years ago. It had come up in conversation that I was absolutely terrified of flying, but I was desperate to go to Australia to visit my best friend. I couldn't see how this would ever be possible as whenever I flew, I would end up physically shaking, crying, and have a panic attack with the slightest turbulence—so not ideal for a long-haul flight!

Susan explained that fear of flying was a fear of dying and encouraged me to think of an instance where I had felt that the world was not a safe place. I couldn't instantly think of anything significant. I had a gut feeling that I was young, so we continued with the process anyway.

My wall was a big brick wall that towered way above me. On the other side I could "see" a valley and rolling hills, a beautiful green landscape. The wall felt totally overwhelming to my inner child, who I felt was under four years old. My child was standing in a sparkling orange ball of light (which I learned afterwards was to do with feelings of disempowerment).

I felt the warmth and love of the angels as they stepped in close. I couldn't help but smile as my child chose a green star for unconditional love, a mauve star for connection, a red star for empowerment, and a gold star for happiness. My child felt loved and secure. I could feel a tingle in my stomach. The wall was much lower—below chin level. She cleared the remains of it away with the wand, and there in front was a beautiful beach with waves lapping at the shoreline and bright sunshine.

It was a beautiful experience, integrating my child into my heart. I felt quite emotional but very happy, and stepping forward into my beautiful valley scene felt right. I felt positive, hopeful, and empowered.

So I left the workshop and felt optimistic about the prospect of flying, and in fact a few weeks later I booked tickets to Australia! The following Easter we flew to Melbourne via Singapore—twenty-four hours in the air! We flew to various other destinations within Australia, and in total I took seven different flights and planes of varying sizes. Not a single tear, not a single panic attack, not an ounce of fear. Utterly unbelievable!

The evening after the workshop, I suddenly had a flash of knowing, and I realised the root cause of my fear. When I was two years old, my brother shut my fingers in the car door—it was so bad that it chopped a piece off my thumb. This was the moment that I realised that the world was not a safe place!

I am so grateful to this process as it gave me my freedom to travel again.

Niall D: [I had] fear of failure from when I was young. The process was very interesting as I felt a huge shift while doing the process ...

The wall holding me back was about head height and showed me an inner child of about 16 years old ... when I acknowledged the child by giving it empowerment and freedom following the process, it changed colour from blue to gold which felt like it symbolised a blocked throat chakra and which freed me from my past ... As this transition occurred, the inner child began to grow and the wall fell. The image the other side of the wall was now visible, and it showed a beautiful meadow with butterflies and a yellow brick road heading into a hopefully and exciting future ... I felt free of the past and walked with the new vision of hope.

It worked and showed me something I did not know was holding me back within my subconscious ... Brilliant process to clear old and outdated patterns.

Petra: I chose to work with the emotional wall process. The theme that I was working with was a sense of protection around my heart and being open to a new love relationship.

When asked how high the wall was, what I saw was a low picket fence surrounding my heart.

When I asked what was on the other side of the wall, my picket fence was actually a circle around my heart. I could see a green field of space in all directions on the other side of the fence.

I realize the word "picket" could also be seen as "pick at", like picking at someone or even myself, but also a picket line, like a protest energy. So my picket fence was founded on reacting against someone or a judging energy in some way to protect my heart.

I could look back at past relationships and see how I was so judgemental against the men I was with and how I now understood that I was protecting my heart with judgment. So, in fact, I have not been accessible or open to connect or attract anyone.

The child that was with me was about five years old. We had a very limited amount of space between our heart and the fence. We could both see that there was open space beyond the fence, and we both could feel we were no longer willing to stay behind the fence. We wanted to knock the fence down and escape into the green field to our freedom. The colour of the child was red, and the colour of me was yellow. The red felt like anger for the child, and for me the yellow was detachment or disconnection from action or the will of my heart—because I was guarding it. My heart was alone and inaccessible.

When I gave the stars of safety, unconditional love, connection, empowerment, freedom, and happiness to the child, we were both able to take action to dismantle the fence. The magic wand allowed us to clear all the debris and build a bonfire and burn the wooden picket fence, thus transforming all the judgement and protective reactions into the openness of love.

This changed how we saw our future options, and we were able to walk into the open field and play together.

When I integrated my inner child with my heart, many tears flowed. Afterwards, my heart felt bigger. I felt softer and more nurturing knowing that my heart was now carrying my inner child and the barrier to the green field was gone. Walking softly and gently into the field, I felt much more sensitive and available. I could experience my body, heart, and soul being together with my inner child.

Reading this last part of the process helped me realize how important it is to allow my inner child to be in my heart and know that she will help me and allow me to connect with a new and sacred love relationship.

"As I walk forward, I let go of the past and move into the present, which creates my future. I will always love and accept you for who you are, whoever you choose to be in this world, and whomever you choose to share your life with. I'm going to pop you in my heart where you will always feel safe, loved, and looked after, and we are going to have so much fun together creating our dreams and living our mission."

Thank you, Susan, for sharing this process.

Alina: I wanted to heal feeling insecure about myself and my weight.

I saw a reddish brown wall. My child was eight and surrounded by yellow. My child felt angry, annoyed that she could not see over the wall. She felt unsafe. After giving her security, unconditional love, and freedom, she was feeling really happy again.

Before I started the session, my stomach felt very heavy and knotted, and after the session felt much lighter. I felt as if some fog had been lifted from my head. For the rest of the days after, I did not stress or worry about what I was eating.

Indra K: A physical symptom, a hardened tissue underneath the physical heart in the diaphragm. The tissue became the wall. It was brownish in colour, thick rubber-like material, hard.

My inner child (3 years) appears on my left side, holding hands with me. She then becomes much younger, about half a year, and appears on my sternum. I can hear her sobbing, and she has her ears on the bone and the area underneath it. She is listening to some pounding and whimpering inside, colour of red. And the feeling inside is so much anxiety and excitement, in a state of high arousal.

When the angel with the star basket appears, she grabs with her tiny hands a sparkling white star. And she's playing with the star—she is engaged in exploring the star, its texture, sound, light. It is flexible, she's almost eating it ... and the wall in the sternum has softened and the tissue underneath is much softer now.

Now, it feels like a connection with the inside of the heart space is established. It still feels like soft white egg but much calmer.

Much relief, and by writing this down twenty-four hours later, the hardened tissue has melted, no pressure. And the message of my heart (space) is playfulness and immense joy.

Mason O'Reilly: I would like to heal my health after being diagnosed with a cancerous lump, then having an operation to remove it. Fortunately, it was successful. I also recently had a potential skin cancer scare but this turned out to be nothing dangerous.

I chose the Emotional Wall process.

The wall started just above head height at the beginning of the process. I was imagining blue sky and a beach. The inner child I imagined was me aged 3–4 years old. The child felt a little nervous, a bit daunted by the wall.

The wall was too big for the child, and I did not get the feeling the child thought much about what was beyond but just stood very close to me.

I put the child in a ball of light—it was silver.

The child was given a star but just felt a bit lost, confused what to do.

The child waved the magic wand given by the angel and after waving it some bricks came down—enough to see beyond it.

The child was now smiling, looking happy. The wall wasn't low enough for the child to see over but was pleased with the effect of waving away some bricks.

When I integrated him into my heart, my heart was beating faster for about fifteen seconds.

I could now clearly see that beach, the blue sky, me sitting having a drink, laughing.

The feeling of relief, freedom, relaxation, happiness.

I am glad I chose to heal my health. It was clearly in my mind, more than I actually realised. It showed me I can see me being healthy and happy in the future.

20

Time Travelling with Your Inner Child and Healing Your Heart

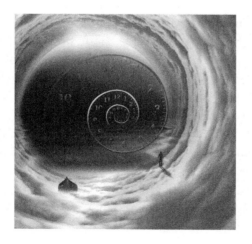

Sometimes we have a specific memory that keeps coming up in our life. These memories we can usually see in our mind's eye. It could be the ending of a relationship, a house move, a childhood traumatic experience, or anything that arises and keeps showing up. This is because it is held as a cellular imprint of memory, and your incredible body is showing you that it has not been healed. This is also held in your vibrational field, and therefore it affects what you are attracting into your life, such as love, health, and money.

You can be a child or adult. Whatever age they are, they will be a younger version than today.

- Place your child/adult in a bubble of protective light.
- Imagine standing next to them as you look today.
- Connect with the emotion of the child/adult self. They may be in shock or fear. You will be able to see it and feel it. Freeze the scene and people within it, except for the aspect of you from that time when you experienced the unwanted event or emotion.
- Bring the angels in, and this time watch as they shower your younger or previous self with sparkling unconditional love, allowing that part of you to heal and feel connected to your inner guidance or, if you would like, to your universal team that looks after you.
- Ask your child/adult self what they need from you and then acknowledge to them this way: "I am so sorry you felt so _____ and there was no one there to hold you and keep you safe."
- Keep doing this until they are ready to integrate into your heart. This will happen when they are fully ready. Keep acknowledging them and letting them know you are honoured that they are here to help you to heal.
- When the younger self is within your heart, you have healed that trauma and perception of belief.
- Sometimes it's important for your younger self to say how they felt to another person involved. If this is the case, go to the Cutting the Ties process in Chapter 22 and follow the process to forgive.

Client Testimonials

Indra K: I wanted to heal the shock and emotions I felt from when I first split from my first love at the tender age of 16 years (after two and a half years together).

These emotions were still affecting me within my relationships today, as they were unhealed, causing insecurity and emotional eating, and not allowing me to fully open my heart, to feel enough and to feel safe to fully shine.

I knew if did not heal the emotional trauma tied to this that I would never feel whole within myself or be fully happy in a relationship, and I would keep repeating this pain.

I was feeling so much shock within my body—high alert, wired emotions, heart beating very, very fast, and in extreme pain.

This trauma and unhealed hurt was also preventing me from moving forward in my business and being fully visible and seen, as I felt unsafe and vulnerable.

I felt that I had to redo this process three times in succession to fully clear the shock frozen within my body from this event. I then tried to go to sleep, as I was doing this late at night, but very shortly after, I realised that I needed to go to the bathroom, and I had a very potent and significant release from the bowels. Constipation is something that I have suffered with a lot in the past, so I knew that this was a very significant act of physically releasing and letting go of that emotional pain that I have held in my body for over thirty years.

I feel more connected to my child self, my teenage self—so young and so hurt.

Bringing that 16-year-old self back into my heart and hugging her tight and letting her know that I am sorry that she had to go through that pain all alone, that I am sorry she felt so unlovable, but that I have her now and I will always be there for her now felt so incredibly empowering.

This part of me was so important to my identity and to me feeling safe and secure in my own skin, to feeling enough and to be able to show up in the world like I need to.

She was crying out for me to acknowledge her, to support her, to encourage her to come out from hiding herself away. That it's OK to be seen. That she was enough and that it was never ever to do with her not being enough. That she was deserving of being fully loved. The part of me that would no longer chase love that didn't choose me.

Thank you so much for the gift of these processes that I will continue to work with to keep healing various parts of me.

Linda Bryan: My goal was to heal the emotions that were causing cancer to appear in my body—the first time as rectal cancer in 2018, and then the second time as endometrial cancer in 2020. Both times I had surgery to remove the affected areas. But I felt my body was trying to tell me something. If I did not heal the emotional trauma tied to this disease, it would just reappear somewhere else.

I was feeling so much grief and sadness from losing my uterus, a part of me that is so strongly connected to my identity as a woman. With the help of Susan and our guides, I was able to shine a light on how deep this emotion actually was and how far back it went. I was 11 when I first lost my identity as a woman. Seeing my mother being beaten by my stepfather made me feel that being a woman was not safe. In addition, I lost my voice because I could not protect her. I grew up with the feeling that women are not protected and their opinions didn't matter. Why would I want to be a woman? Once I realized all the fear, anger, grief, sadness, and resentment that I was holding in my body, it was time to clear it. This began with many apologies to my 11-year-old self.

I cried a lot through this process. Bringing that 11-year-old self back into my heart felt so amazing. I did not realize how important she was to my soul and my identity. She was that energetic part of me that was shouting, "I'm not being heard! It's not safe to be a woman!" This is why I was being shown these messages in my body. These were the cries of my inner warrior princess. Healing that 11-year-old part of me was a big step towards making choices based not on fear but on feelings of empowerment.

P. Marsden: Issue to heal—setting boundaries with my father, not automatically doing what he says without considering how I feel about it.

I saw my 4-year-old self being held upright, aloft on one of my father's hands (which he used to love doing at any social gathering). I felt really scared he would drop me, and I couldn't trust him to look after me. I did the process and my inner child showed me she was right not to trust my father at that time, as he had inadvertently hurt her whilst cutting her nails. She showed me that I needed to talk to her more as she remembers what I need to remember, and protecting her was protecting myself now. She reminded me that I was now 51 and not 4, and I didn't have to do what my father says if I don't feel it's for my highest and best good.

Fiona Ritter: I choose the unmet need in my childhood. For me, there was no one I could speak to in safety and trust.

I saw my inner child immediately—she was waiting for me In a shy manner, and as soon as I had put her into the bubble of protective light and the angel's with unconditional love came in, she became more open, alive, and trusting. I could feel her in my heart space, and that was my anchor through the process. I reassured her many rounds, holding her hands, and she told me everything she had felt about living in that family and its very frightening atmosphere. She sobbed, was in tears; many layers from within came to light. I felt that there were many helpers from the angelic world to clear the turbulent family energies out of my cells.

I feel much more easy with myself, especially in my heart—it is more expanded. Also relieved, and the adult within me asked, "How can I be a better mother to my inner child today?" I feel confident that more of my unmet needs come to light to be healed.

21

The Projector Process

This process is fabulous for taking energy out of you and seeing it clearly on a screen.

Think about something that stops you once again, and this process will help you to release the blocks held in your field. This can be particularly helpful when we can't access our emotions but can imagine a colour.

- Imagine a white screen in front of you or to your side.
- Project the colour onto the screen that is inside you. Use the Colour Energy Clearing chart in Chapter 18 to help you.
- If the colour could speak, what would it say?

- Imagine that there is an archway of light within that colour, and observe your little inner child.
- How old is the child standing in the archway or colour?
- Connect with what it is in front of you on the screen.
- Use the angels with the other processes to heal the aspect of you that is showing itself, and integrate it within your heart.

Client Testimonials

Annabelle: I've used the Projector process several times for different things. It always gives me new insight and awareness into each issue, and helps me to see it from a wider perspective. It also helps to highlight what emotions are involved that need clearing. I find it very helpful in shifting me out of a negative headspace around an issue into a neutral or positive frame of mind.

One example of when I used the Projector process was in regards to my occasional (but very debilitating) migraine headaches. The emotions that came up for me during the process were confusion and frustration, as well as sadness and weariness. Through the process, I was able to heal the emotions and to see migraines through a more neutral and even hopeful lens. With the confusion and frustration gone, I now knew that there was a holistic answer to this painful problem. Later that day, I finally found the herb combination that has helped to heal my migraines from their root cause instead of just covering up the symptoms.

The Projector process has become a great healing tool for me to use on both emotional and physical issues.

Yvette: I did the Projector to help me with some lower back pain. I fell on my tailbone one and a half years ago and I'm still hurting. I can't bend over without pain. So I thought I'd give the Projector a try.

Several colours came up for me, and many emotions with visions of my husband came up in my life during several conflicts we had. My younger self was there but in a foetal position—as if trying to protect herself, is what I got. I got a little emotional and then brought in the angels to help clear this and just saw so many stars sparkling around. I stayed here for a while, then when I felt I was done, I anxiously stood up and bent over—and for the first time in a year and a half, I bent over with no pain! Oh my gosh, how wonderful!

Thank you so much! I can't wait to do another one of these processes!

22

Cutting the Ties that Bind with Forgiveness

This process has shown to clear old contracts, past lives, instantly heal marriages, help divorce or heal without needing divorce, heal mother or father relationships or relationships with bosses, work colleagues, and even abusers.

Why is that, you ask?

We are all connected, and the relationships that show up outside us that bother us are actually a mirror of our own lack of self-love, anger resentment, fear, loss—whatever emotion shows up. When we heal these, our vibration has more light, and therefore we show more love out to the world and the world shows it back. This process will release you from old patterns and relationships. You can even cut the ties with those who have passed over to spirit.

- Imagine a person here or in spirit with whom you would like to heal your relationship. Remember, this is just to cut the ties that bind, that don't serve you, not the loving bonds or marriages in this life—unless of course they are no longer for your highest and best good.
- Ground yourself using Earth Star*Soul Star, then invite the person to join you in your mind. You are connecting with their soul, and they know that this will help them too, so don't worry about asking them—it's not needed.
- As you look at them and they look at you, how do you feel? What emotions come up for you?
- It's not your job to heal them, so we will do that for you. Imagine in front of them a beam of pure light. Imagine them stepping into this light and receiving pure connection to Source, unconditional love, and whatever else they need. If you prefer, just hand it over and know that they will receive exactly what they need to heal.
- Notice now how you feel when you look at them.
- Has something changed for you?
- Next it's time to cut the ties that have bound you lifetime after lifetime, stopping you from being free.
- Say to them, "Today from a place of unconditional love, I choose to set myself free, and as I do this, I set you free too. I choose to forgive myself as I choose to forgive you. I let go of anything from any lifetime, past, present or future that does not serve us. I choose to release any pacts, agreements, vows, oaths, marriages, religious orders, blood bindings, chains, sacrifices, written and verbal contracts, and any lifetimes of slavery or feeling trapped in any way, in any timeline or

lifetime. I do this with unconditional love deep within my soul."

- Check in with how you feel now. What has changed?
- Then say their name and "I feel _____"— whatever you want to say that you haven't been able to say. Really speak from the heart. For example: "I feel that you have made me wrong, betrayed me, hurt me."
- From a place of unconditional love, say, "I am setting us free."
- Watch them float off, or you can bring them into your heart.
- If it is a current relationship, you can always ask the true soul reason for why you are together, the mission you have.
- Watch what happens.

Client Testimonials

Alina: I wanted to heal my relationship with my son. I have always been very close to him. For the last few weeks I felt really distant from him. I felt like he was avoiding me and excluding me from his life.

During the process I felt he was really disappointed with me. After putting him in a beam of light made up of unconditional love, security, and freedom, he was smiling at me again.

Immediately after the process I didn't feel so angry with him anymore. The strangest thing is after a few days we had such a heartfelt conversation, our bond has strengthened even more.

Claire Terry: This is a beautiful process, both powerful and gentle. As I watched my sibling step into the light, she was showered with a light filled with different shades of pink, which for me symbolises unconditional love. As I continued to watch, layer after layer was falling off her, and she looked so happy.

I felt such love for her, and I knew that our relationship had been healed and forgiveness was fully present. Thank you so much.

Deb Neshi: I chose this process knowing I had a lot of unresolved emotions from personal relationships that needed clearing.

I tried this process today. I innocently thought it was a matter of two or three people that I needed to forgive. I started the process with my mom, then Dad, etc. As I was doing the process with each one of the expected persons, other people from old relationships kept popping up. It was as if the process itself was reminding me of other relationships that I was not consciously aware of, and of other people that I needed to forgive and also to forgive myself for. After about one and a half hours of the process—lengthy because so many other relationships had come up for clearing—I was having trouble breathing, as I was crying so much. After a while, feeling calmer, I was very thankful that I was able to clear a lot of those old, leftover emotions. I felt a lot of healing and clearing, and I felt lighter and brighter.

The process is very easy and it goes deeply, almost surreptitiously. I found it to be an unexpectedly very insightful and helpful process. I will revisit it soon. I know throughout our many lives we have collected many stuck emotions, just for being human.

Big thank you to Susan and her Divine Team.

Wendy: With great anticipation, I tried the Cutting the Ties that Bind with Forgiveness process with my dad, and it did not disappoint! I did this process with the intention of healing and freeing myself from any anger, resentment, or frustration I've felt towards my dad. After connecting to my dad's soul, I looked at him, and he seemed lost. There was such a sense of confusion and loneliness in his energy field. Some tears ran down his face, and I teared up as I felt such compassion for him.

I pictured him in a beam of light throughout the process and trusted that he was receiving just what he needed for his own healing. As I followed each step in the process, I knew that this was the right process for the right issue, and I spent a particularly long time telling him how his choices made me feel. Finally it was safe for me to speak freely, and I took full advantage of it, LOL.

When I've tried having discussions with my dad in person, his anger and "it's my way or the highway" attitude prevented me from being able to finish my sentences, leaving me to feel voiceless and powerless, not to mention dismissed, disregarded, and diminished as a woman and especially as his daughter. I backed off of our relationship considerably because of this. After trying this process about a month ago with another family member and instantly experiencing a positive change in our relationship, I decided it was time to use it with my dad for my own healing, inner peace, and freedom.

I felt such relief wash over me as I spoke my mind. I expressed all of my feelings about how his choices have impacted me. Thanks to Susan and this process, I was finally able to unburden my soul from the anger I had picked up from him my entire life. In the end, I expressed my love and then sensed my dad's relief as I set us both free. It felt great ... I feel great! Whether my dad makes any changes in his communications and relationship with me or not, I have experienced an internal shift that will serve me well.

23

The Mirror Process

The Mirror process can be used on its own or with the Emotional Wall process after releasing the wall to access your higher self.

- Imagine walking up to a full-length mirror. Stand in front of it.
- What do you see?
- Sometimes you will see just light. (If you see just light, then you can see that your energy field is utilising and holding more light.)

- You may see yourself looking unhappy or another vision of yourself—you will see what you need to heal.
- If you see yourself with unwanted feelings in the mirror, step away from the mirror. Invite your angels and guides to come in and fill you with light to heal that aspect.
- Step in front again. What has changed?
- Sometimes you may see something in the future—for example, pregnancy, family, a home, or even better your mission, why you are really here.
- If it is something that you wish to hold, then see this as a picture. Bring the picture to your heart, and feel that energy flow through your body to integrate this vision.

Taking it a step further, you can ask your Higher Self to show themselves. Step away from the mirror, and then fill your body from head to toe in beautiful sparkling light. Then step in front of the mirror again. This is your higher self.

Ask your higher self to talk to you and have a conversation about anything you need to know. If you are ready you can step into the mirror and fully align to your light body, your true soul self.

Client Testimonial

Katy: I did this process as I wanted to heal the current situation in my relationship. My boyfriend's ex has come back on the scene, and she has mental health issues and is very emotionally unstable, and he is tied into the situation with trauma and guilt. He needs to cut her from his life and had committed a hundred percent to me; however, since she has contacted him, he is unable to at the moment because of his guilt, as she is very unwell and he feels responsible for her.

When I looked into the mirror, I saw a very elegant version of myself, like a lady of the manor or chateau, wearing a very long and glamorous emerald-green ball gown. My hair was dark, glossy, with big and bouncy curls. I feel it could have been me from a former life.

The second part of the process, I saw a beautiful, opaque, iridescent light with a rainbow spectrum of colours running through it and on the outer edges. I knew this was my higher self.

The third part of the process, when I stepped through the mirror, I felt like I was flying. I was on the back of a huge bird. I think it was a snowy owl, but huge. I was high above my life, looking down on it from a bird's-eye view.

I asked the reason why I am experiencing this situation with the ex.

I got that it was for me to fully step into my feminine divinity. To fully relinquish my power, my goddess energy.

It's like I was looking down on him and summoning him up with my finger: *Look I'm up here, I'm up here shining. I like having you there as a prop. But can you keep up, little boy? Have you got what it takes to meet me up here?*

It's like he and this situation in my life have given me the push to really shine. To learn to let go, trust, and surrender, toss my ego aside and fully concentrate on me. To be whole within myself. Fully secure within myself. To be steadfast in my life, in my goals, in my work. But it's a test to see if he can rise up to and overcome his block, his obstacle—which is to put himself first and realise he can't save or be responsible for anyone. To be in the driving seat of his life and create what he wants rather than let guilt control him. Is he man enough?

I feel great about it. I feel strong and in control now. I can see why this situation is happening for me—not *to* me. For my growth. For me to step up to improve myself, not for me to sink down. Because what I have to offer to him is amazing and he can see it. But if he can't step up and reach me, if he's not brave enough to break out of his prison of negative emotions, then he is not for me. He can stay in his unhealed unhappiness, but I am off to pastures new!

Thank you so much for these amazing processes.

24

Soul Rebirthing

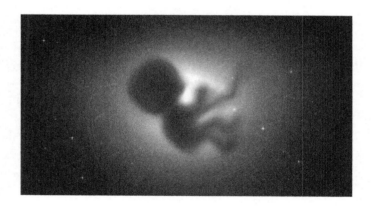

Soul Rebirthing is a process that takes us back to the point of conception and heals any unwanted trauma or perceptions of belief that you may have held right up to your birth. In healing these traumas, you will feel free and clear and ready to step fully onto your mission with excitement.

To prepare for this process, come into your heart, breathe, and imagine listening to your heartbeat. Then you can follow step by step to connect with your baby self.

- Close your eyes and imagine you can go back to the point of conception.
- Connect with the light at the point of conception. How does that aspect of you feel about coming into the world? Use colour energy clearing to understand the colours and emotions, if you need to.
- Bring in a beautiful angel with a magic wand for the soul, a cloak of protection to place around the light, the Akashic records[1] so they have everything they need within, a crown of sovereignty, and a basket of stars full of love, connection, and whatever your baby self needs. Trust with this that your baby self has everything they need.
- Travel throughout the growing in the womb. Stop at every point that is needed—you will be guided. Clear any dark energy or fear with the magic wand and the help of the angels. Use golden sparkling light or platinum wherever needed.
- When ready, imagine the tunnel being lit, and being born to yourself. This is a birth of ease and grace; you are recreating your birth even if the one you knew was traumatic. This one will be peaceful and full of light.
- Put the baby in a beautiful bubble of light and place them into your heart. Feel the love and reconnection.
- You have just recreated your beginning. Enjoy the newness in your life.

Client Testimonials

George: I felt that I wanted to heal being hard on myself and the feeling of judging myself.

It was beautiful. I felt an instant connection to birthing the soul doing the process … The light was golden and white, and I had a fear

---

[1] The Akashic records are the inner knowledge of lifetimes before you remember who you are: a being of light.

112

of disconnecting to unconditional love, which was coming from my mother and my soul during the initial birth which I transformed. ... Once I birthed myself again using the process, I felt completely free again and could feel my solar plexus tingle as I calibrated myself back to complete unconditional love for myself without judgement ... a very empowering process.

It has given me the feeling that it just turned into something much deeper and transformational. Thank you.

Jackie Smith: I wanted to heal relationship to self, feeling disconnected, and disappointment about being female.

It took me a week before I could do this process on myself because it just felt too painful. I was really afraid that I would become overwhelmed. However, I also trusted the work I had done with Susan and therefore knew it would be OK to do this process on myself. I just had to trust myself with the process. I went onto my timeline all the way back to that point of conception.

Immediately I felt trepidation, anxiety, and a deep heaviness. The colours were dark grey, brownish greens. I remembered to send light to the colours and sparkles to break up the dense heaviness. As I did this I felt a huge sense of relief, like someone had switched on the light inside the womb!

As I moved along the timeline, I felt a pull at about four or five months old. I had a sensation of being curled up tight, so I surrounded my baby self with soft light fluffy clouds, creating a sense of buoyancy. I felt lightly massaged by the clouds, allowing me to gently move and stretch. I invited an angel to help with the process. The angel gave a wand and beautiful magenta cloak of protection which completely shifted the energy into feelings of empowerment. It felt very liberating.

Then again I felt a pulling sensation at eight months. This time the angel gave me a star for courage, a star of unconditional love, and a star for connection. Knowing that I had the cloak of protection and the stars, I felt ready to be birthed.

As I saw myself being born, I surrounded myself with golden-pink sparkly light, and automatically she went deep into my heart with ease. I could feel the tears rolling down my face as I felt this deep connection to myself as a baby feeling safe, secure, and loved.

Before the process, I felt confusion, separation, and disconnection, but afterwards I felt a shift in my perception of me and how I felt about myself. I now have this deeper knowing that I am worthy, I am loved and loving, and I am now honouring being female! I really didn't expect to have these amazing insights and sense of relief. I am so much more accepting of myself and my experiences.

Having done this process and spent some time reflecting over a week, I have noticed that I feel more present in my body. It feels more comfortable to be in my body. I am so grateful for that too.

25

Infinity Process

Use this process to visualise and quickly clear energy with a person, situation, or place.

- Imagine you are standing in one loop of the figure eight or infinity sign, and the person, place, or situation is in the other.
- See the figure eight spinning, and set the intention that the block or resistance is released. You may see it disappear, if

that is something that is for your highest and best good, or you may see it turn into light. If it is light, then imagine the whole figure eight inside your heart.

- Breathe and smile. It is done.

26

Forgiveness Letter

Dear Angels,

Please help me to love and forgive myself.

Dear Self,

I am deeply sorry for not listening to you, my inner child, and for not realising that all you needed was my time and love.

I am sorry for criticizing you when all you needed was love.

I am sorry for being busy when all you needed was a little peace.

I am sorry that you believed all those things you were told even though they were not true.

I am sorry that when I looked in the mirror, I saw imperfection instead of love.

I am sorry that I blamed my body for letting me down when all it was doing was helping me see I needed to love myself more.

I am sorry for not listening to my soul and what my true mission was.

I am sorry I gave away your power to others and didn't respect you.

Please, Angels, help me to love myself and my inner child more.

In deepest gratitude for this opportunity to be human,

Yours truly,
[your name]

AFTERWORD

So now you have great tools you can use to connect with your soul and your individual mission. You have powerful processes that you can use again and again to heal any part of your life.

Thank you for journeying with me and my team of guides to help you heal. They have a few last words for you.

We hope you can feel our love and adoration for you, and please remember you are never on your own. You do not walk this path on your own. We are always here to love, support, and guide you, and we are grateful that you chose to experience being human this time. You are part of the unified heart, the unified field of light; we are all one.

We send you blessings, love, and light, assisting you on your journey to continue to awaken the light within your heart.

ABOUT THE BOOK

We are in the midst of massive global change. And while so many unknowns lie ahead for humanity, it's clear we all have an opportunity to heal and step fully into the life we came to lead. In fact, it's necessary for us to do this inner work so that we can show up and create the monumental change this world is craving and needing.

In a transformative guide, Susan Kennard relies on her experience as a therapist and medium to lead others through profound, yet easy-to-follow processes to release blocks from the past that include unwanted childhood trauma, limiting beliefs, and old energies in order to awaken the light within and align with a destiny and true identity. Kennard shares stories of her own personal awakening and healing journey; offers insight from her guides about relationships, money, freedom, and even animals and how they help us heal; and provides guidance on how to clear past traumas and open a path to healing.

Awaken the Light within Your Heart shares personal stories, insight from spiritual guides, and a transformative process that encourages healing on a deep level.

Printed in Great Britain
by Amazon